THE FACE OF

Baseball

PHOTOGRAPHY
AND PLAYER PROFILES BY
JOHN WEISS

WITH AN ESSAY BY
WILFRID SHEED

THOMASSON-GRANT
CHARLOTTESVILLE, VIRGINIA

For Sara
An All-Star in any league

Published by Thomasson-Grant, Inc.
Designed by Gibson/Parsons Design
Edited by Owen Andrews and Rebecca Beall Barns

Printed in U.S.A. by Progress Printing, Inc.

97 96 95 94 93 92 91 90   5 4 3 2 1

Inquiries about the photographs should be addressed to:
John Weiss
Department of Art
University of Delaware
Newark, DE 19716

Library of Congress Cataloging-in-Publication Data

Weiss, John, 1941-
   The face of baseball / photography by John Weiss ; with an essay
by Wilfrid Sheed
      p.   cm.
   ISBN 0-934738-59-9
   1. Baseball players—United States—Biography. 2. Baseball
players—United States—Portraits. 3. Photography of sports.
I. Sheed, Wilfrid. II. Title.
GV865.A1W43   1990
796.357'092'2—dc20
[B]   89-49059
                                               CIP

Thomasson-Grant, Inc.
One Morton Drive, Suite 500
Charlottesville, Virginia, 22901
(804) 977-1780

(Page 2) Cincinnati Reds look
at U. S. Army skydivers, July 4, 1984.

TONY ARMAS
AND HITTING
INSTRUCTOR
TOMMY HARPER

5

"WHIP-O"
FUNGO BAT

I. THE AGE OF THE FACE

**THE
GAME
THAT
NEVER
ENDS**

by
Wilfrid
Sheed

*S*ince the coming of television, baseball has been preeminently a sport of faces: long ones and round ones, Nordic and Latin and African ones, and even a solitary Japanese who came and went—a veritable smorgasbord of faces, imprinted on one's brain by the endless North American summer and the relative stillness of the game, and by the eternal browsing of the TV camera. By the time the season reaches the September crunch, your favorite team is family, as familiar as an old photo album, and its good news is your good news; its pain, your pain too.

It wasn't always like that. Once upon a time, only

the cream of the cream of ballplayers had real faces; the rest only had approximations. Babe Ruth could draw a crowd anywhere, but most of his teammates might have marched down Broadway unrecognized; while if, say, a second-string catcher had any features at all, that was his own business. What we did know by heart in those days, if we were lucky enough to see any big-league games at all—which leaves out most of the nation—were the players' stances and styles and mannerisms, which had to tell us all that their expressions tell us now. (Any fan my age can easily do you a DiMaggio, or a Musial, or a Mel Ott; just hand him a bat and watch out for the furniture.)

Perhaps a measure of how far the Age of the Face

OREL
HERSHISER

has come can be taken from the booming traffic in baseball cards these days. When I was a child in the forties, 12 years old was about the cutoff point for dealing in these things. After that, there was little to detain you; the writing on them was primitive, and the pictures were worse than passport photos—you felt as if you knew more before you looked at them. Yet now, even those old monstrosities are worth something, as our new hobby reaches back to the past for more faces to feed it.

But obviously we should be able to do better than bubble gum cards to immortalize this and future generations of baseball players. If we really want to know what these fellows look like (and right now I

OZZIE
SMITH

TOMMY KELLY, SON OF
TWINS MANAGER TOM KELLY

KEN DAYLEY AND
RED SCHOENDIENST

13

can't think of any public faces that interest us more;
our politicians have never looked so drab, and movie
stars tend to be nothing *but* face) we need some
baseball portraitists right now—the game's very own
Steichens and Avedons, who happen to love and under-
stand this one profession well enough to read their
subjects' thoughts and catch their moods on the fly.

Which brings me to John Weiss, whose work adorns
this book, and of whom I will say right off that he has
the best bedside manner of any photographer I've ever
encountered, and one so well adapted to ballplayers
that he could wring a smile out of Sad Sam Jones, or
a tear from Laughing Larry Doyle, or their modern
counterparts. (In the eternity of baseball, all the
players have counterparts.)

MIKE
BODDICKER

15

MIKE
KRUKOW

MARK CRESSE, DODGERS COACH
AND BATTING PRACTICE PITCHER

17

John's deployment of pictures in this book is a
fair depiction of his working methods. The first photos
are mostly medium close-up, get-acquainted shots, in
which one can sense the photographer taking his
man's measure—noting how the subject holds himself
and what he does with his hands; and incidentally
winning his unspoken permission to move in closer
and become his friend for a few minutes.

With these preliminaries out of the way, Weiss
closes in for the kill, the hasty rummaging among
eyes, mouths, and noses to find where the man keeps
his soul, and then to steal it double-quick before the
subject wakes up. And if this sounds too dramatic, you
should see John work, prowling forward like an Indian

KEITH
HERNANDEZ

19

scout and mesmerizing his victim with chit-chat. "So he's thrown you nothing but curves all day" snap "and the bases are loaded in the eighth" snap "so how long can you wait for the fastball anyway?" snap. "Come on—I'll bet you looked better than that on your honeymoon." Snap, *snap*. (I made this up after listening to him—his own stuff is better.)

Interspersed among these shots one finds a third, more highly evolved group. In these, John the photographer clearly knows his guys well enough to move back again, further than before, without losing their essence, and to capture them in context with each other and with their habitat of dugouts and playing fields. These pictures seem to relax and expand and

FERNANDO
VALENZUELA

LEN
DYKSTRA

22

DARRYL
STRAWBERRY

GARRY
TEMPLETON

LARRY
BOWA

become part of the great flux of baseball, "the game that ends, the game that never ends," as the Englishman Herbert Farjeon wrote of baseball's elderly relative, cricket.

To complement this, my text will start with a fan's long shot, as he first enters the stadium, and then move in closer, with a fan's mind, that jumble of awe and curiosity, to get a better look. And then out again into the flux.

DAVE
WINFIELD

MIKE
GREENWELL

28

2. THE DREAM

*F*orget what you have seen on TV; nothing in life so far has prepared you for that first squint down the ramp—at the impossibly green grass and the golden patch of infield and the figures in white moving across it. It is your first glimpse of perfection, and from then on even the rank smells of mustard and grade Z beef will be transubstantiated by it, and the hum of the crowd will sound like a choir of angels, every time you enter a ballpark. And perfection only becomes more so as the home team explodes out of the dugout and the play begins.

It is a great stage set, of a kind that extracts

CARLTON
FISK

30

LOU
WHITAKER

31

prolonged applause from first-night audiences and, incidentally, sets certain writers to gibbering whenever they hear the word baseball. Rumor has it (rumor, Hell—I've felt the damn stuff) that sometimes they use fake grass these days, and that certain infields have been reduced to white lines and postage stamps of dirt—but not here. This writer is such a fanatic on the point that he actually believes Ping Pong should be played on grass too; so there will be no Astroturf in this essay.

Because Astroturf, for all its chemical charm, is not the stuff that dreams are made of, and this is a book of dreamers. Every face in here, from the most cynical to the most trusting, has dreamed the Dream early and

PAUL
MOLITOR

33

often, starting in Peewee League, where our hero

first hitched up his pants and learned to spit like a

professional, on up through the lower depths of pro

ball where the lights are barely fit to read by, or maybe

the college ranks where they use tin bats to save

money (Charles Dickens would have thrown up his

hands at the stinginess), and everywhere buses—not

glamorous trains with parlor cars or airplanes with

stewardesses you can marry later, but regular, down-

at-heels, no-frills buses, bumping along exactly the

same as they did in the Depression when they carted

the elite of the nation's bums and sharecroppers to

their next appointments; a means of transport so

boring and uncomfortable that you are almost forced

to dream in self-defense.

MIKE
EASLER

 35

And all the dreams could probably be filed one way or another under the words "big league": big-league baseball dreams, of course, but as the bus grumbles its way through the night, no doubt visions of big-league meals as well, not to mention big-league girls in big-league hotels, and, for the pure of heart, even a big-league house for the parents. Playing in the minors must be something like serving as an intern in an inner-city hospital or doing the dirty work in someone else's law office: all you can think about is having your own practice uptown someday. And for a ballplayer uptown means Yankee Stadium, or something like it; that is to say, a ballpark you can remember even from the television snippets and not

DWIGHT
EVANS

(LEFT TO RIGHT) JOE COWLEY,
ED WHITSON, AND PHIL NIEKRO

FLOYD RAYFORD WITH RICHARD JUSTICE,
WASHINGTON POST SPORTSWRITER

39

LOU
PINIELLA

40

GEORGE
"SPARKY"
ANDERSON

one of those anonymous sports factories that turns
into a football stadium every time you turn your back.

   Yankee Stadium is particularly dreamworthy
because, not so long ago, the World Series used to turn
up there as punctual as Wimbledon, and by the time
the bus reaches Altoona, our hero is undoubtedly deep
into the seventh game of some future classic. No one
has yet taken a poll of rookies' fantasies, but young
guys reporting for duty in the Bronx for the first time
have been known to go into something like shock upon
finding themselves standing where Babe Ruth stood in
right field, or DiMaggio just in back of second, or
Gehrig at first. (To compare lesser things with greater,
I once sneaked out to center field myself as a youth to

ANDRE DAWSON

43

see how things looked from Mickey Mantle's point of view and felt the same tingle some people get from Civil War battlefields.)

Ballplayers have a sense of history like no other athletes, if only because baseball *has* a history, and not just a collection of famous names and faded photos. A football player has nothing to measure himself against because his game is constantly changing and obliterating its past, so that if you asked one how to defend himself against, say, Ernie Nevers or Steve van Buren, he'd probably wonder who the devil you were talking about, and why. But a young pitcher today who's so minded can easily imagine throwing to Jimmy Foxx or the Babe; we not only know exactly what their swings

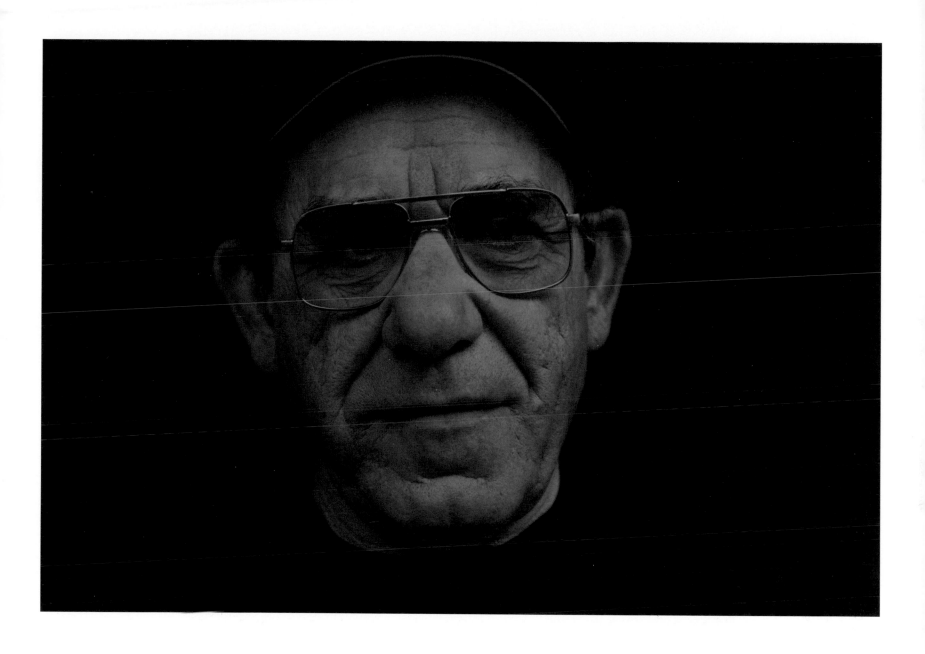

YOGI
BERRA

45

STEVE
GARVEY

WILLIE
RANDOLPH

47

looked like but what kind of pitchers they hit best.
And we know their statistics so well we can almost see
their faces in them. Everything in baseball is recorded,
down to the meanest sacrifice bunt, and the records
still vibrate. When Pete Rose broke Ty Cobb's record for
base hits, he wasn't competing against some antiquity
or curiosity; that was a real barrier he had to run
through, made of real base hits, and everyone on the
field including the bat boys knew it.

Which is not to say that everyone in this book has
a head stuffed with numbers, or is even a baseball fan.
(Just last week as I write this, Mookie Wilson, the
exuberant ex-Met, was reported saying, "I could never
watch that stuff, I have to play.") Ballplayers come in

DAVE
STEWART

many shapes and sizes. But the flakiest of them knows that this is a sport in which the word "immortality" actually means what it says, and doesn't expire every five years or so. When Ted Williams drops in on a spring training camp, he doesn't have to introduce himself—and neither would Ruth; they are baseball royalty and always will be. And a young player might reasonably figure that if he too hopes to go down in history, he might as well know what history is. Politicians who wish to be remembered almost invariably become students of history, just to get the feel of the stuff. And the aforementioned Pete Rose probably knows as much about the past as a history major or your average U.S. president.

ANDRE
THORNTON

51

DON
SUTTON

KIRBY
PUCKETT

And speaking of Rose, the man is also walking, or running, proof that studying history is good for the soul, because it has left him with at least one pure desire, stronger even than his desire to get back in the game professionally, or to cash a triple exacta; strong enough possibly to make him a living saint if necessary—and that is his craving to be enshrined in the Hall of Fame at Cooperstown, the baseball equivalent of Abraham's Bosom, or Valhalla, where the game's heroes live together forever along with their impedimenta of gloves and bats and hats.

Now there is a museum for you. If the measure of such places is their ability to bring a whole civilization to life, item by item, so that you can practically hear the

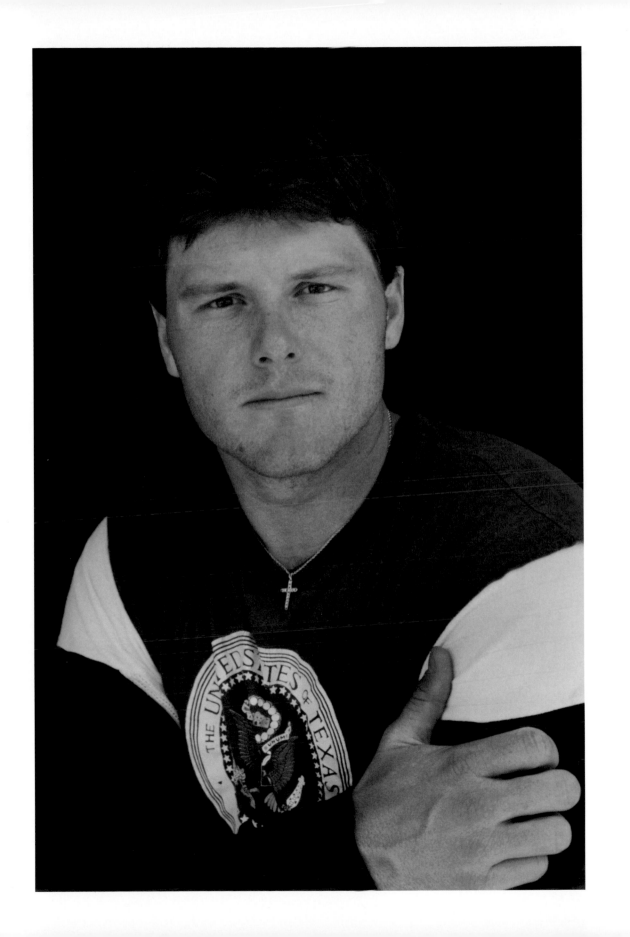

ROGER
CLEMENS

55

CHRIS
SPEIER

 56

PHILLIES TRAINER JEFF COOPER
WITH JEFF STONE

57

THE PHILLIE PHANATIC'S KISS
(WITH OREL HERSHISER)

STEVE GARVEY'S KISS

crowd sounds and feel the atmosphere on your skin,
then there is no more thorough one in the world than
this unpretentious hideaway in the middle of nowhere
in upper New York State. Although I am no believer
either in ghosts or the movie *Field of Dreams*,
Cooperstown is different; I would not only expect to
hear voices if I got locked in there some night, along
with the clack of spikes on the floor, but would have
a crisis of faith if I didn't.

So this is the pot of gold, the coronation, that lies
at the end of the road for ballplayers who do their job
well, and although ballplayers—young ones at least—
probably are not as sentimental as fans, slavering over
bric-a-brac, everyone in this book has probably given
Cooperstown at least a thought. And the neat thing

TONY
GWYNN

about it is, you don't have to be a Grand Master to get your foot in the door; one hitting feat allows your bat in for you, and an errorless streak can do the same for your glove. Or you can enter as a team. Each of the great or just plain unusual outfits has a glass case to itself, so all you have to do is make sure you belong to one of those. Or failing anything else, just wear an unusual sweat shirt or use a bottle-shaped bat like the (very) late Heinie Groh and hope for the best—nothing related to baseball is too small for the museum's generous attention.

And finally, for those who can't even get a sock or an unusual belt buckle in the Hall, there is still a form of immortality to be had even by you, because baseball also has its own Good Book, in which your deeds are

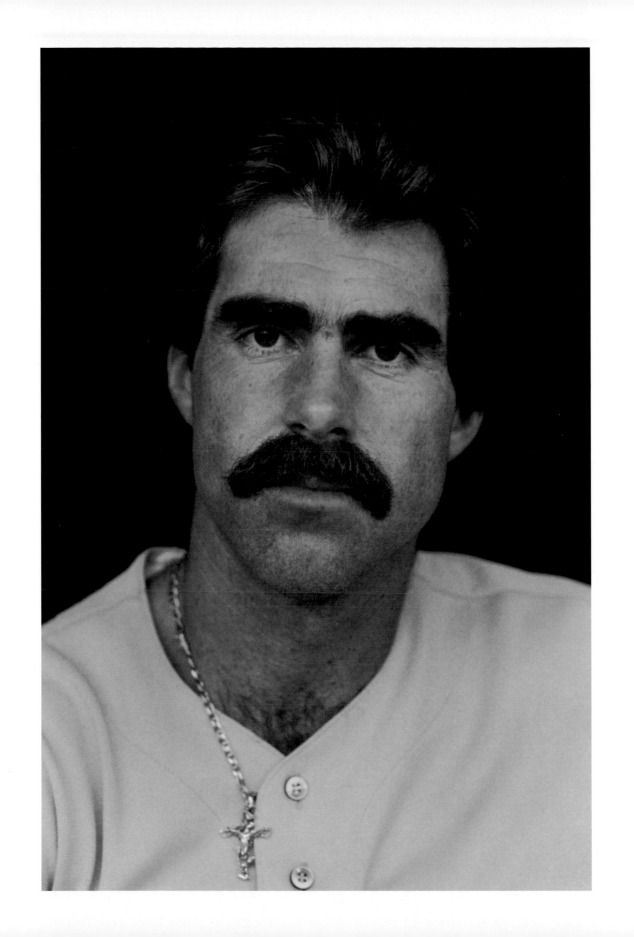

BILL
BUCKNER

63

DAVE
SMITH

BERT
BLYLEVEN

65

inscribed forever, or at least as long as you and print
and baseball are around to care. Whether your name is
Aaron or Zwilling, whether you have been to bat in the
majors 10,000 times or just once, there it all is in the
Baseball Encyclopedia to be discovered and committed
to memory by insomniacs yet unborn. (In fact, if you
change your last name to Zyzmanski, you might even
find your name mentioned in essays like this.)

So. If the first sight of a major league ballpark is
daunting to a fan, imagine for a moment how it must
look to a rookie, with all this in front of him; the noise
is deafening and the lights must seem blinding, brighter
than high noon, and the moment he steps out there, he
knows that the meter will start running on his record,
his shot at glory. One of the actors from the movie

VIDA
BLUE

TIM
RAINES

68

MIKE
FLANAGAN

69

Major League reported afterwards that he had never experienced such audience pressure; and that was just from performing in front of a few thousand people that the producers had rounded up to fill one grandstand; and that was just make-believe.

So imagine further the unbridled glee of the rookie upon discovering that this atmosphere actually suits him, and that this is just the place for him to be; as he trots out into the noise and glare, he is coming home and going to work all in one, and he will be checking into this office every night for a long, long time to come. "It's great to be young and a Giant" said the aforementioned Larry Doyle back in 1912. And then, as now, he said a mouthful.

KENT
TEKULVE

JUAN
SAMUEL

72

3. THE DREAMERS

Watch a troupe of basketball players loping through an airport sometime and you'll think you've died and woken up in Flamingo Park; turn them into football players and the scene becomes a convention of night-club bouncers. Sharing an elevator once with a group of both types, after a party for Joe Namath, I felt I was alternately gazing up Mount Fuji and being crushed to death. And I found myself wishing that Joe only knew a few baseball players, so I could get my bearings.

In other words, ballplayers, alone among Big Three athletes, come in regular Earth-sizes that the ruck of us can identify with and dream along with. The Elias

PHIL NIEKRO

74

KEN SINGLETON
(LEFT) AND
JIM HUGHSON
TAPING PREGAME
COMMENTARY

75

(LEFT TO RIGHT) KENT HRBEK,
TONY OLIVA, AND JOHNNY PODRES

(LEFT TO RIGHT) CHARLIE O'BRIEN,
BALTIMORE POLICEMAN, AND DAVE MCKAY

77

Sports Bureau reports that they are currently two inches taller than they were 50 years ago, but then maybe we all are; at any rate, they don't need to be. Lenny Dykstra of the Phillies looks as if he would fit in your pocket, yet I have seen Lenny hit impressive home runs, while his former teammate Howard Johnson hits them "over buildings," in Casey Stengel's happy phrase, with a physique that looks like precisely the national average.

Gazing round a specimen locker room (the San Diego Padres'), I get the impression that the pitchers may be responsible for the extra two inches; but even this is traditional. The legendary John McGraw, on whom even movie baseball managers are based,

ROLLIE
FINGERS

79

DWIGHT
GOODEN

FRED
LYNN

wouldn't look at a pitcher under 5' 10", which would be six feet now—presumably on the same principle that prompts groundskeepers to raise the mound at times in the interests of a dominant home pitcher, so as to exaggerate the downward swoop of his pitches (purists: check the difference between Dwight Gooden on a high mound (L.A.) and a flat one (Chicago)).

Other judgments vaguely attributed to McGraw, who was kind of a Poor Richard's Almanac of baseball smarts, were that "pitchers are not ballplayers" and "ballplayers are not athletes," and even if my memory made one of these up (my heaviest baseball reading occurred at the age of 11), old photographs would seem to bear out both propositions. Scrawny, bowlegged,

DENNIS
BOYD

DENNIS
MARTINEZ

84

JULIO
FRANCO

potbellied—no physique was too bizarre for some of the old-timers, Ruth included. It seems as if the only way one could tell they were ballplayers at all was that they couldn't possibly have played anything else.

This is only glancingly true today. The likes of Kirby Puckett among outfielders and Rick Reuschel among pitchers are probably as eccentrically designed as ever, and all bets are off with catchers, who still reserve the right to look like fireplugs. But in general, today's ballplayers are manifestly athlete-athletes, with well-tended physiques and wholesome faces, who could easily pass for track stars or squash players and not just for the first team at McGonnigle's Saloon, as their forebears usually did.

ROBIN
YOUNT

MIKE

SCHMIDT

88

PETE
ROSE

Two revolutions are responsible for the change, the first happening forty-some years ago when baseball pretty much gave up on daylight and became a sport for night people. One by one the wrinkles disappeared from the players' faces and their eyes re-emerged from their eternal squint: and they automatically began to look a good ten years younger—although a few, like Robin Yount, continue to look as if they've fought in five different wars, on both sides. (On the other hand, some also took to stumbling around under fly balls like blind men when they were obliged to play in the sun: "better," as an old Brooklyn Dodger might have put it, "they should sleep in coffins all day.")

The second revolution occurred just the other day,

AL
HOLLAND

and if one had to put a name on it, I'd say Steve Carlton, with Nolan Ryan seconding. The sight of these two aging flamethrowers outliving their spans, like creatures in mythology, snapped baseball's head around on the subject of conditioning. Up to then, players had tended to view this issue with superstitious caution. "Very few injuries are caused by falling off bar stools," said Casey Stengel, who was the fountain of wisdom in residence through the forties to sixties, and, incidentally, the linear heir to McGraw; and the great Joe DiMaggio made virtually a fetish of avoiding exercise in the off-season, and had every injury known to man to show for it. In those days, hunting and fishing might be okay if you were a fanatic. But weightlifting,

PHIL
NIEKRO

93

TONY
PEREZ

BOB
BOONE

95

the current rage, would have been unthinkable: you didn't need all those muscles, in fact they got in your way, and no one had yet come up with a method, prior to Nautilus equipment, for touching up muscles selectively. So perhaps the Nautilus people deserve a footnote of their own in the Baseball Encyclopedia for their contribution to that unheard-of phenomenon, the 40-year-old superstar.

Sitting, or rather, standing, in the clubhouse (civilians sit by invitation only), I am struck by how much the personnel resemble young executives arriving for work. The fact that many of them are black passes unnoticed by now, either by them or by me: in fact, I only thought about it later, because people always ask you about

WILL
CLARK

AUTOGRAPH SESSION,
MEMORIAL STADIUM, BALTIMORE

(LEFT TO RIGHT) OREL HERSHISER, TOMMY LASORDA, STEVE SAX, PEDRO GUERRERO, AND TOM NIEDENFUER REACT TO THE PHILLIE PHANATIC

KENT HRBEK AND
BERT BLYLEVEN WRESTLING

KEVIN GROSS AND LARRY ANDERSEN
DURING RAIN DELAY

101

race, and it occurs to me that the outside world has been infinitely slower to integrate than the supposedly less real one of sports.

What one does notice, though, is that the players are better dressed, in more expensive-looking clothes or even suits (for lunch with their publishers no doubt) than the guys I used to wait for outside the Polo Grounds and Ebbets Field years ago. These are not workmen clocking in for duty, but relatively wealthy young men—some wealthier than others, but nobody seems to worry about that. There is next to no class resentment around here because these guys are dreamers through and through, and each of them hopes to hit it big himself someday. So Orel Hershiser won the jackpot this year. Great. Maybe I'll get mine next.

LANCE
PARRISH

The other danger that was feared when free agency was established in the seventies and salaries flew through the roof was that players with that much insulation from life's chances would dog it, subconsciously or otherwise, and this may have happened in a few cases; but it is in no wise epidemic. The Dream was never primarily about money anyway, but about playing baseball in Heaven, and this the guys still do with the abandon of kids playing for nothing. I can't remember ever seeing more home-plate collisions than I have this past year, and you would never guess from watching these simulations of train wrecks that the legs and arms tangled up in there are worth millions of dollars apiece.

DWIGHT GOODEN AND
RON DARLING

KENT
HRBEK

ERIC
DAVIS

107

All the same, today's players are probably cooler customers than their forebears. They have spent less time in the minor leagues getting broken in to their trade, and on average, more time in college. And free agentry has tended to make them free lances, whose attachment to the team they play for is strictly year to year and renewable (though it's amazing how intense it can become in the course of a single season; a championship team is like a platoon that has come through a long war intact, buddies forever). If they fight and scratch eyes less than they used to, it's partly because they have less riding on each other than they used to— and partly because they simply don't see as much of each other as they used to. The heat of train

RICH
GOSSAGE

communication has given way to the coolness of air travel, and it's possible for a selfish player to live entirely inside his own skin, treating his locker as a private office and his teammates strictly as business associates; and it's possible for one or two such misplaced yuppies to sink a team without a trace, or be suspected of it (e.g., the New York Mets—at least the "suspected" part).

Yet even these flowers of the eighties are nothing new to baseball, which has seen it all by now, several times over. The Selfish Player is as old as the game itself, and what's interesting is that there are so few of him these days, considering the temptations. After the haggling of winter has ceased and the dismal rattling

KEN
SINGLETON

JIM
RICE

TOM
SEAVER

of coins, and after the last agent has slunk from human sight, most of the players revert happily to type. Once they're out of their million-dollar sports shirts and into their monkey suits, you wouldn't know them from Ty Cobb or Lefty Grove or the characters in Ring Lardner, except that the pants are tighter these days, and the physiques look better maintained; these are ballplayers, a species as unmistakable and indigenously American as buffalo, and even the century doesn't matter much.

Leaving the clubhouse and entering the field, Weiss and I come upon a bunch of Phillies cavorting around the batting cage. Roger McDowell, the sinker-ball pitcher and world-class cut-up, is at the center of it, and McDowell has a tendency to reduce, or elevate, things to the sandbox level wherever he goes. So the

OZZIE VIRGIL JR. AND SR.

115

GARY CARTER (LEFT)
AND ROGER MCDOWELL

(LEFT TO RIGHT) ATLEE HAMMAKER,
ALEX TREVINO, AND ROB DEER

AL NIPPER'S BUBBLE

 118

JUAN AGOSTO

players laugh as they bunt and jockey each other like frat brothers around him.

Somebody points out a lady in red who comes to watch batting practice each day, and whom they've nicknamed "The Cat Lady," and Weiss says, "I'll bet she only comes to see you, Roger." And McDowell dimples prettily and says, "Well, she's only human."

And so is he, and so are all of them.

DAVE
PARKER

NOLAN
RYAN

 122

*E*very age in baseball is a golden age, and this one is no exception. Old-timers complain that players today are not as steeped in baseball as they used to be, and make more mental errors, and this may be true. Those long hours on the train and in the pre-television hotel lobby were mostly spent talking *base*ball, *base*ball, *baseball,* to the sound of train wheels and the whir of overhead fans, while the extra years in the minors were like the equivalent in violin practice; the old players were note-perfect at their craft and could throw to the right base, or hit behind the runner, in their sleep, where they sometimes were (day games left you a lot of time to play at night).

Yet the best of them probably never fielded more infallibly than Keith Hernandez or pitched more shrewdly than Orel Hershiser or hit more knowingly than Wade Boggs. If the average of competence is lower these days, the peaks may be slightly higher, as today's geniuses avail themselves of technological aids that simply didn't exist in the other golden ages. Tony Gwynn, the young master, is famous for traveling with a tape deck full of pitchers, and of himself hitting against them, which he studies before each game (unlike some of his free-swinging colleagues, Gwynn also uses the batting cage as a lab); while Davey Johnson, the Mets manager, would be lost without his computer. A student of the game has much more to

CAL SR., CAL JR., AND
BILLY RIPKEN

DOUG
DECINCES

STEVE

BEDROSIAN

study these days, and the bull sessions between catchers and pitchers, batters and coaches, and slumping players and anyone who'll listen, are correspondingly more nutritious.

But this is merely garnish. No one has built a computer that comes close to matching Casey Stengel's head (1890-1975) or Keith Hernandez' today. A good baseball mind comes with a built-in feature that computers will never have, namely, hunch-capacity or the instinct that tells a great card player to go for it on this hand regardless of the data, or a manager to switch to a left-hander against a right-hand hitter—or, as famously happened once, to bring in a hungover old Hall of Famer to pitch with the bases loaded in a World

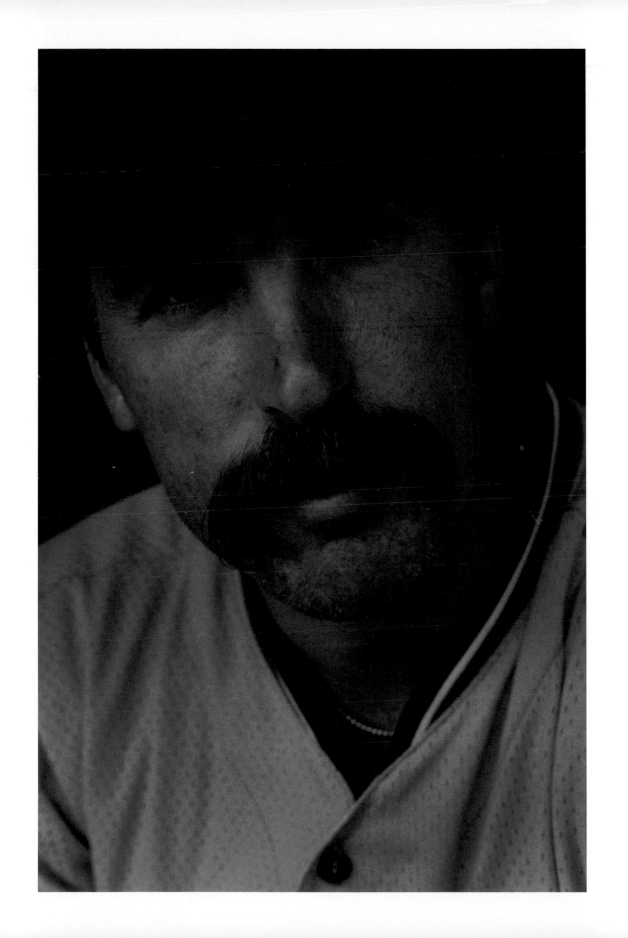

JACK
MORRIS

Series. It would take the manager all day to explain the move, even to himself, but half of a split second to know it's the right one.

And while such accurate illuminations may actually be so rare in cards that it might be wiser to ignore them, they are the very essence of baseball, with its constant fluctuations of circumstance and profusion of possibilities. A computer might, for instance, know exactly what a given batter is likely to do in every conceivable situation—where he hits curves, where fast balls, and how both against this particular pitcher— and still not know that his bat looked slow on that last pitch—maybe from the heat wave, or from worry about his divorce (gossip helps at times), or just from thinking

WALLY
JOYNER

AUTOGRAPH SESSION,
FENWAY PARK, BOSTON

 132

WALLY JOYNER

KELLY GRUBER

(LEFT TO RIGHT) DON ZIMMER, JIM FREY, AND TONY KUBEK

too much; and that's just to list his problems—you should hear the pitcher's.

The good baseball mind has all this stuff and more stored where he can get at it, faster than an Epson could print it out: and on the strength of it, Hernandez or Ozzie Smith or Willie Randolph moves back just a few feet—just for this pitch. When and if the count goes to three and one, or two and two, it will be a whole new ball game, and he'll have to rethink the situation (while the computer collapses with exhaustion).

Now more than ever, intelligence *is* skill in baseball, and glancing through John Weiss' cast of photographs, I am impressed by the sheer brain power assembled here, a veritable thinktank and powerhouse of baseball

RYNE
SANDBERG

137

cunning. Orel Hershiser's brain cells alone, when turned on full as they were at the end of the 1988 season, could light up a whole city block if one knew a way to plug them in.

But I am also impressed by the sheer animal talent and pure physical skill of these particular men. No baseball fan is happy unless he gets to pick an All-Star lineup now and then, and it was my intention to end with one now, drawn from this book—one that I feel I could match confidently against any squad from any time in the past. But I found myself completely defeated by the position of shortstop. How in God's name does one leave out Ozzie Smith? Or Cal Ripken, Jr.? Or Alan Trammell? Or the Robin Yount of 1982? And then

ALFREDO
GRIFFIN

WADE
BOGGS

MARK
MCGWIRE

there's the Mike Schmidt vs. Wade Boggs problem at third...Okay, that goes to Schmidt, but what about Lou Whitaker and Ryne Sandberg at second? Or Clark and Hernandez at first?

Managers have to make hard choices in cases like this, but I don't. Because John Weiss also had the vision to photograph the best manager in baseball, Sparky Anderson (no argument about that) and, as I see it, it's his headache now.

All a fan has to do at this point is what he was put on earth to do: heckle, and admire.

CAL
RIPKEN JR.

(LEFT TO RIGHT)
MIKE FELDER,
PAUL MOLITOR,
AND JOEY MEYER

 144

AFTERWORD

By JOHN WEISS

THE TUNNEL was about 50 yards long, carpeted, with walls of cinderblock. Overhead, jutting out from a hole in the wall, was the back end of an air conditioner, which was set on groan and rumble. It was quick-dripping onto the carpet. Of course, the carpet was soggy and dank, but there was another, fouler odor: the faint smell of cat urine, masked unsuccessfully by an extra-strength disinfectant. It was an altogether horrible place, and I couldn't have been happier, because the light at the end of this particular tunnel beckoned me, for the first time, onto the playing surface of a major league baseball field.

As I stepped out of the gloom and onto the spongy Astroturf at Veterans Stadium, home of the Philadelphia Phillies, I had no idea I was beginning an odyssey that would carry me across five seasons and to nearly 200 games. All I knew was that my heart was pounding wildly, and I hoped that I didn't seem too conspicuous, too much the hayseed.

I can tell you that the color green was invented just for this moment. Before me, the smoothest, most shimmering sea of green I'd ever seen seemed to stretch toward infinity. Astroturf may be hard on the knees, but at 2:33 P.M. on May 22, 1984, it was mighty easy on the eyes.

If the plastic rug is distinctive for its vibrant color, it is also peculiar for the odd sound a fast-moving baseball makes as it strikes the surface. Like a silencer on a Magnum .44, the turf reduces the sound of a hard-hit ball to a dainty little "ping," instead of the mighty thwock one expects. As I stood there watching and listening to the sounds of the Phillies taking batting practice, I still felt like an interloper. But I also knew that I was where I'd always wanted to be, that I was at home.

BATTING PRACTICE is baseball's most time-honored pre-game ritual. "BP" seems a loosely organized activity, but in fact has a definite shape, its own precise movements. It is a social event—a time for conversation with teammates and for hellos and howdys to players on the opposing team—as well as a time for working on one's craft. It is a formally orchestrated concert with room for improvisation.

Each team gets the field for 50 minutes, and every hitter is permitted an exact number of swings. Standing at opposite ends of the batting cage within painted circular borders, two coaches hit ground balls to the infielders. There is a lovely, syncopated rhythm to this ritual, the coaches pausing until the batter has hit the ball, then quickly moving into action, swatting fast-hopping grounders to a waiting infielder, then pausing again for the batter to hit, then smacking grounders once more, repeating the sequence over and over. And meanwhile, in the outfield, pitchers are stretching, playing "long toss" to loosen their arms, and running laps along the most distant perimeters of the field.

Standing behind the batting cage is the team's hitting instructor, deeply focused on the mechanics of each batter's swing, oblivious to the dozens of civilians roaming about: newsprint reporters, radio announcers, TV personalities, technical staff, public relations and promotion employees, photographers—sometimes nearly 100 noncombatants. Most everyone is engaged in a series of brief conversations. About the only time the talk stops is when one of the game's great power hitters—a Reggie Jackson or a Jose Canseco—steps into the cage. Then things get real quiet real fast as one of these sluggers begins pulverizing the soft, straight batting practice pitches, launching them into high orbit, the

ball getting smaller and darker until it disappears over the distant outfield fences. After a particularly prodigious shot, there is an audible intake of air, followed by whoops and shouts and finger-pointing by

John Weiss photographing the Ripkens, Memorial Stadium, Baltimore, 1987.
(Ellen Weiner)

those gathered, while in poetic counterpoint, the batter feigns a portrait in studied nonchalance. "I didn't quite get all of it," he might say, shaking his head ever so slightly.

Of all the major league teams, no club is more organized or more competent in its approach to BP than the Los Angeles Dodgers. They are the only team to always use a batting practice *catcher* (Mr. Todd Maulding of Rancho Cucamonga, California), the theory being that with the benefit of a target, the pitcher will throw more strikes, thus giving the batter more good pitches to hit.

No one is more essential to the Dodgers' efficiency than their batting practice pitcher and coach, Mark Cresse. As the opposing team is about to complete its workout, Cresse waits, poised just outside the foul line, ready to sprint to the pitcher's mound to begin work. In his left hand is a huge blue box, resembling a footlocker, filled with dozens of practice balls. And bulging out from his back pockets are even more baseballs, for immediate access the instant he reaches the mound.

It was my good fortune that the Dodgers were in town during my first visit to the Vet, and my doubly good luck to come upon the rear quarters of Mr. Cresse. Just as I was about to snap the shutter to make what would become the first picture for this book (see page 17), Jose Morales interrupted the shot by sticking his bat into my field of vision. His intrusion only served to make my original idea a thousand times more interesting. Morales' bat not only introduces a wonderful graphic parallel to the foul line, it accentuates the shape of Cresse's stuffed and overburdened pockets.

Later in that 1984 season, when the Dodgers were back in town, I gave Mark Cresse a copy of the photograph I'd made. From that moment on and for the next four years, whenever Mark saw me coming, he'd turn precisely 180 degrees and point his posterior in my direction, just to be sure I could recognize him.

THOUGH IT WAS great fun to be on a major league diamond where I could observe, close-up, the amazing skills these players brought to the game, my intention was to photograph them in a way that would reveal a sense of the person, not the superstar. I had no interest in the bubble gum facade or the glossy and exaggerated televised exterior. I hoped, instead, to express a more fundamental aspect of each of my subjects: something substantial, essential, primary, in the face of each man.

A working pattern soon emerged. My home in Delaware is only an hour's drive from Philadelphia and Baltimore, so I could photograph both National and American League players as they arrived to play either the Phillies or the Orioles. I'd get to the ballpark around 2:30 in the afternoon, a full five hours before game time. After setting up my "studio"—a black background cloth taped to the dugout wall, a patch of reflective foil taped to the dugout ceiling, and a stool placed in front of the cloth—I'd go to the visiting team's clubhouse to scout for players I wanted to photograph. I was after the top three or four from each team, and it wasn't unusual for the best players to be among the earliest arrivals.

Convincing the players that my project was legitimate was far easier after I had accumulated a set of finished portraits. Sometimes, as I was showing my photographs to a particular player, others would gather around to peek. These were fun times. Ballplayers take great delight in razzing one another, and as I'd turn to each new portrait, I could always count on someone shouting, "Mullion!"—an epithet not described in my Webster's, but which clearly means that someone is beyond ugly, that the face should be covered with a bag, that a viewer could go blind looking at it.

When a player agreed to pose, I'd escort him to my dugout studio with no specific plan of how to photograph him. However, certain physical characteristics often suggested a visual starting point. For instance, Rollie Fingers' luxuriant moustache demanded a straight-on, full-face approach, while Andre Thornton's massive arms, Mike Easler's taped fingers, and Andre Dawson's expressive hands each invited special emphasis. The portrait session would last from five minutes to half an hour, depending on the player's endurance or the level of skill I brought to the sitting that day.

If the photographs produced from a sitting were beneath my standards, I did not hesitate to admit as much. I'd return later that season or the next to ask the player to pose again. And if the second meeting was equally barren, I'd go back for a third try, or even a fourth if I was convincing enough.

Each encounter was distinctive. Each portrait session was personalized and made memorable by the quality of interaction. Most were pleasant; some decidedly were not. It's appropriate, then, to conclude this Afterword with the remembrance of five such experiences.

"I LIKE YOUR PORTRAITS," he said. "Would you take one of me?"

I was in the Dodgers' clubhouse and had just finished showing my portfolio to several players, when this long, tall, skinny kid, about 21 years old, I guessed, asked me to take his picture. He was wearing dress pants, but was stripped to his waist, revealing a chest so sunken a squirrel could have nested in it. He had on the kind of plastic-framed glasses you might buy off the shelf at the local five-and-ten. His polite, almost deferential manner made him seem like the boy next door, the nerd you'd visit only when you needed help with your math homework.

But even though he clearly wasn't a ballplayer, my policy at the ballpark was to photograph anyone who asked. We agreed to meet later in my dugout studio. When this "kid" showed up, I was truly staggered by his physical transformation. Walking toward me dressed in full uniform regalia with the confident and easy grace of an athlete, glasses replaced by contact lenses, the number 55 and the word "Dodgers" on his shirtfront, was the 26-year-old rookie pitcher, Orel Hershiser. The metamorphosis was complete; he looked every inch a certifiable major league ballplayer.

As a portrait subject, Orel was as baffling as he was agreeable. He was willing to attempt any pose, but I was unable to find anything remarkable in his face. It seemed unexpressive: too pleasant, without weight. Nothing worked in that first encounter; I couldn't bring him alive for the camera.

The frustration continued through three more sittings over the next two seasons. Finally, in 1986, a spontaneous gesture led to a photograph worthy of our effort. I gave Orel two baseballs to hold and was thrilled to discover how they accentuated the gargantuan dimensions of his hands. And when he crossed his legs and cocked his left wrist, his torso tilting slightly forward, something magical happened. Now his face, his posture, his persona suggested the substance of the man. They combined to express an inner strength, a sense of the vitality and passion that is Orel Hershiser.

ANDRE DAWSON is known as "The Hawk" for his fleetness afoot, his ball-catching skills, and the way he attacks a baseball. But that moniker can also apply to the cast of his face, for he presents a forbidding countenance, his face set hard. He can be an intimidating presence.

I wasn't at all put off by that exterior, and from the moment Dawson agreed to my portrait request, we were at ease with each other. It turns out that Andre Dawson is simply a quiet man, comfortable with himself, thoughtful and self-contained. He told me he is well aware of what his face seems to say to the world, but to his mind that is a misleading statement. He doesn't feel hard or mean; he is simply a serious soul, a man intent on the task before him: preparing mentally to win a ball game. With Dawson, it is a matter of professional pride to bring absolute focus to his work.

As I began to photograph The Hawk, we discussed how to deal with the issue of his hard face. I suggested he get as comfortable as possible, let happen whatever happened and said to think about hitting "a five-run homer." My stupid little joke was just enough to provoke a laugh (you had to be there, believe me) and gave me the courage to attempt to lead Andre into some difficult poses, to take a few creative chances.

The portrait sitting developed into a true collaboration, and the resulting image is an absolute favorite of mine. Rather than conveying any note of meanness, Andre's face suggests a personal power both compelling and comforting, a sureness which combines with his easy elegance to infer a man of character and depth.

JIM RICE acts the bully. I had the chance to observe him seven or eight times during five seasons, and saw him as quite a consistent fellow: tough, confrontational, surly.

He was no charmer with me. As I approached Rice in the visitor's clubhouse in Baltimore, intending to make my portrait pitch, he cut me off in mid-step before I could speak, shouting sharply at maximum volume: "NO!" I understood in that instant that this was an intimidation tactic, and though I felt like a bullet had creased my ego, I continued walking toward him, hoping that I hadn't broken stride, that I hadn't betrayed my discomfort.

Nevertheless, Rice agreed to look at my portfolio and then agreed to pose. When he sat before my camera, a truly amazing transformation took place. As I pointed my lens at his face, Rice's angry disposition evaporated, just melted away before my eyes, and was replaced by a new attitude: buoyant, invigorated, incandescent, as "turned on" for the camera as anyone I've photographed. He was a delight. He was easy. Jim Rice had given me a gift.

HE AGREED to take the cigar out of his mouth, but Vida Blue wouldn't take off his cap and he wouldn't sit still. He was teasing me. I was trying to shoot his portrait, and he was reciting aloud the writing on my camera lens: "50 millimeter, 1.8, Canon, Japan." He was having the best time subverting my attempts, while trying to hide his uneasiness at being photographed. Despite my best efforts, I shot a lousy roll of pictures that day.

When the San Francisco Giants returned to Philadelphia the next season, 1986, I was determined to get Vida to pose for me again. He remembered me, we shared a laugh over his photo-antics, and he quickly agreed to sit for another session.

I knew this session would be different, because after some initial reluctance, Vida finally took off his cap. It was no great surprise to discover that his forehead traveled a significant distance toward the base of his skull before it was interrupted by hair. Vida had simply been vain; now we were over that hurdle.

This time the sitting went well. Vida was still a delight to be around. The photograph that emerged was a mirror of the time we shared; it portrayed Vida as I saw him—a hint of a smile on his lips, animation in his eyes, and a warm and reassuring radiance illuminating his face.

I BELIEVE THAT every baseball book should have a Yogi Berra story, and mine happened in Baltimore in 1984.

I was at Memorial Stadium to photograph the Yankees when I spied Yogi, then the Yanks' manager, sitting in the dugout. I stopped in my tracks and blurted out a request to shoot his portrait, and Yogi gave me the go-ahead. I snapped off a few frames, but Yogi was uncomfortable and wouldn't hold still;

he kept turning away from the camera to follow the pre-game action on the field. It was nearly 7:30, and since press aren't allowed in the dugout so near to game time, I was worried that I'd be kicked out at any moment and would miss my chance.

In desperation, I hollered, "Yogi, you're moving around too much. Please look straight into my camera." And Yogi responded, a warm grin lighting up his face, "Oh, no, I can't do that. That's my bad side."

Well, Yogi is seldom wrong, but this time he was. Full face, straight into the lens, is indeed Yogi's best side. His face has a genuine, if unconventional, kind of beauty. His is a kind and amiable face, an open face, a face without guile. And best of all was a note written to me by Carmen Berra, Yogi's wife, saying the portrait was "the best one yet."

So, thank you, Yogi, thank you, Carmen, thank you, Baseball, for letting me share in this wondrous continuing saga which fascinates and unites so many of us from all across society. I hope that my pictures humanize the men who play our national game, these sometimes brittle, always captivating American heroes. I truly hope my work honors the game, the men who play it, and the fans who watch over it.

PLAYER PROFILES

By JOHN WEISS

With Commentary by
Mike Flanagan and Keith Hernandez

Additional Comments by
Dwight Evans and Tom Herr

Steve Bedrosian
(page 127)

"'Bedrock' is the epitome of confidence out on the mound. Of course, it helps that he has a 95-mile-an-hour fastball to go along with his nasty slider." (KH)

Nicknamed "Bedrock" not only in joking reference to the Flintstones' neighborhood, but also for the solid, reliable quality of his pitching, Bedrosian was one of the leading relief pitchers of the 1980s. He was named National League (NL) Rookie Pitcher of the Year by *The Sporting News* in 1982, and won the Cy Young Award in 1987 when he led the league with 40 saves for the Philadelphia Phillies. Traded to the Giants in 1989, he became San Francisco's "stopper" and helped lead the team to the NL pennant. Bedrosian has 161 career saves.

Yogi Berra
(page 45)

"Everyone knows that Yogi is one of the all-time great baseball characters. Some of my favorite stories, of course, are 'Yogi-isms.' For instance, there's the story about the pie. Supposedly, Yogi walked into a bakery wanting an apple pie and the lady behind the counter asked, 'Well, how many pieces do you want me to cut this into?' And Yogi said, 'You better cut it

into four; I don't think I could eat eight.'" (MF)

Yogi Berra was not merely one of the greatest catchers in baseball history; he set some records which may never be equaled. Berra hit 358 career home runs, had 1,430 RBI, and struck out only 415 times in 7,555 at bats. He caught nearly 1,700 games in his 19-year career, and was voted to the American League (AL) All-Star Team for 15 consecutive years. Berra played on more pennant winners (14) and more world champions (10) than any player in history. He owns the World Series records for most games, at bats, hits, and doubles, and is second in runs scored and RBI. He was the AL Most Valuable Player three times, in 1951, 1954, and 1955.

Following his retirement, Berra was hired as the Yankees' manager in 1964 and guided the team to a pennant that year. He has worn a major league uniform for 45 years, mainly as a Yankee, but also as a New York Met, and, most recently, as a coach for the Houston Astros.

Vida Blue
(page 67)

"He could throw bullets. He jammed me so bad on a cold night in San Francisco that he dislodged a nerve in my left thumb, and I have to wear a sponge on the thumb to this day. He just pounded people inside, inside, inside. It was like he was saying, 'Here it comes—let's see you hit it.'" (KH)

In 1971, Vida Blue had one of the most sensational rookie seasons in history. He won 24 games, recorded 301 strikeouts, and led the AL in shutouts (8), ERA (1.82), most strikeouts per nine innings (8.68), and fewest hits allowed per nine innings (6.03). Blue was such a baseball phenomenon his first season that attendance in Oakland and in all AL cities increased markedly whenever he pitched. For his accomplishments, he was named his league's Most Valuable Player and won the Cy Young Award. Pitching primarily for the A's, and later for the Kansas City Royals and the San Francisco Giants, Blue had three 20-win seasons. He retired in 1987 with a lifetime record of 209-161.

Bert Blyleven
(pages 65, 100)

"What's unique about Bert is how often he's been beaten down and how he's always come back stronger than ever. He's a guy who refuses to give in. He'll have a bad season and come back the next and be nearly unhittable. And his curve ball is amazing. When Bert's 'on,' even the best hitters will swing and miss by a full two feet." (MF)

Armed with one of the most devastating curve balls in the game, Blyleven has recorded 271 victories in his 20 years as a major league pitcher. He followed one of his poorest seasons in 1988 (10 wins, 17 losses, 5.43 ERA) with one of his best in 1989, turning in 17 wins, 5

losses, and a 2.73 ERA. And in the same year, at the age of 38, Blyleven surpassed Walter Johnson and Gaylord Perry in all-time strikeouts to rank fifth with a total of 3,562. With 60 career shutouts, he leads all active pitchers and holds ninth place in baseball history in that category. Blyleven has won 15 or more games in 10 different seasons.

Mike Boddicker
(page 15)

"No matter what the score or how big a lead he might have, Mike wants to bury you from the first pitch of the game. He's not blessed with tremendous overall ability, but he's got an amazing knack for deceiving hitters by mixing his pitches." (MF)

Boddicker's 16-8 record during his 1983 rookie season helped lead the Orioles to a World Series Championship. He topped the AL in shutouts that season (5) and was named the Rookie Pitcher of the Year by *The Sporting News*. Boddicker won 20 games in 1984 but had only one winning season in the next four years. Traded to the Boston Red Sox in 1988, he regained his form in 1989, compiling a record of 15-11.

Wade
Boggs
(page 140)

"It seems you have to throw Wade Boggs six pitches for his every at bat. I think his game plan is that the more pitches he forces you to throw, the more likely you are to make that one mistake. When he finally gets his pitch, he'll usually hit a line drive with it. He has an incredible knack for hitting the ball where no one is at." (MF)

Wade Boggs will be remembered as one of the best hitters of the 1980s. Since his rookie year in 1982, Boggs has won five AL batting titles, including four in consecutive years (1985-88). He is the first player in history to have four straight 200-hit, 100-walk seasons (1986-89) and the only one in this century to have 200 or more hits in seven consecutive seasons. Criticized early in his career for erratic fielding, Boggs has developed into an excellent third baseman and led the league in double plays in 1984 and 1987. His lifetime batting average of .352 was far and away the best in baseball in the 1980s; he led his nearest competitor, Tony Gwynn, by 20 points. Boggs is noted as well for his superstitions, including his habit of eating chicken for good luck before every game.

Bob
Boone
(page 95)

"Bob Boone epitomizes what a catcher should be. I have admired him for years from the opposite dugout. It seems that wherever Bob Boone goes, the pitching staffs always do better." (MF)

In 1989, Bob Boone set a record by catching 100 or more games in a season for the 15th year. He is the all-time leader in games caught with over 2,100, and has won six Gold Gloves while playing for the Phillies, the Angels, and the Royals. In 1986, at the age of 39, he finished second in the major leagues in games caught. At the age of 41, he had the highest batting average of his career (.295) and led the AL in assists by a catcher. Boone is much admired for the way he "frames" home plate, setting his target and receiving the pitch so that the home plate umpire perceives borderline pitches as strikes.

Larry
Bowa
(page 25)

"He's one of the game's great competitors. Cocksure, temperamental, he's the kind of guy who tees you off when you play against him, but the kind you want to have on your team." (KH)

An almost flawless fielder, Bowa established several major league records for the shortstop position, including highest lifetime fielding percentage (.980) and most years leading the league in fielding (6). His fielding percentage of .991 set the single-season record for excellence in 1979. Conventional baseball wisdom suggested that Bowa would never amount to anything as a hitter and that this deficiency would prevent him from having a long career. But Bowa converted himself into a switch hitter and proved his critics wrong by collecting more than 2,100 big-league hits. He reached a single-season high of .305 in 1975 and averaged a very respectable .260 for his career.

Dennis
'Oil Can'
Boyd
(page 83)

"He's one of the great characters of the game. He packs a lot of motion into a 140-pound frame. I really couldn't believe that a pitcher could get so hyped-up on the mound and continue it for 35 starts — a whole season. On the day after he pitched, I'd look at the outfield during batting practice expecting to see him collapsed, but there he'd be, playing basketball and running all over the place. He just has a tremendous amount of energy, and you have to give him credit." (MF)

Dennis Boyd's nickname was given to him in his youth by beer-drinking friends in Meridian, Mississippi, where beer is referred to as "oil." Depending on your point of view,

Oil Can is either one of the most delightful characters in baseball or an infuriating hot dog. He regularly refers to himself in the third person as "The Can."

Boyd's career got off to a promising start with the Boston Red Sox. He won 12 games in 1984, followed by 15- and 16-win seasons in 1985-86. However, a series of career-threatening injuries, most notably blood clots in his pitching arm, have placed his career in jeopardy. In Boyd's three healthy seasons, he averaged 228 innings pitched per year. In the three seasons since, Boyd totaled only 224 innings. The Can was able to return to the mound late in the 1989 season and win three games, reestablishing hope for his baseball future.

Bill
Buckner
(page 63)

"He played in pain all the time. I agonized to watch him. We never talked hitting, but just from watching I could follow his plan of attack. I liked to watch him hit more than anybody else." (KH)

At the end of the 1989 season, Bill Buckner had more hits than any other active major league player (2,707). Buckner began his distinguished career 19 years ago as an outfielder with the Los Angeles Dodgers. Later, he played first base, most notably with the Chicago Cubs. His mobility has been terribly slowed by severe ankle injuries in recent years, but the young and healthy Buckner was a heady base runner who stole a career-high 31 bases in 1974. Buckner led the NL in hitting with a .324 average in 1980 and has batted over .300 seven times in his career.

Will Clark
(page 97)

"Will's going to be the next premier player in baseball, if he isn't already. He's very intense, a strong personality, the type of guy who will always be motivated to be the best. This is difficult in these days of big money and heavy pressure. But you can give him a five-year contract and know he'll play his butt off and earn every penny." (KH)

After playing only 65 games in Single A-ball in Fresno, Clark made the incredible jump to the majors in 1986 and hit a home run his first time at bat. He has developed into the most feared all-around hitter in the NL. In 1988, he became the first player in the history of the San Francisco Giants to play in every game in a single season; he also led the NL in RBI and was voted to the All-Star Team for the first time. Clark finished second in batting in 1989 with a .333 average, stroking 23 home runs and driving in 111 runs. After four big-league seasons, Clark's career batting average is .304, with 98 home runs and 352 RBI.

Roger Clemens
(page 55)

"What makes Clemens special is that he not only has overpowering ability, but great knowledge of pitching to go along with it. I think he'll be the dominant pitcher in the game right through the mid-1990s." (MF)

Nicknamed "Rocket Roger" for his 95-mph fastball, Clemens set the major league mark for most strikeouts in a nine-inning game with 20 in 1986. That same year, he won 24 games and lost only 4 and led the AL with an ERA of 2.48. Clemens won 20 again in 1987 and received the Cy Young Award in both seasons. Though slowed by injuries in the last two years, he was still the workhorse of the Red Sox staff, pitching over 250 innings each season and winning 35 games during that time.

Ron Darling
(page 105)

"He's a man in search of himself: a very complicated man. He's a bright guy, constantly thinking, but sometimes, it seems, to his disadvantage. Maybe he overthinks. It just seems every year he gets into a rut, gets himself in trouble, and has to pitch his way out of it. When he stops messing around, stops trying to nibble, he starts to win." (KH)

A winner of 87 games in six big-league seasons with the New York Mets, Darling has never won fewer than 12 in a single year. His best season was in 1988, when he had a record of 17-9 and set a personal standard with four shutouts.

Eric Davis
(page 107)

"If he stays healthy, he could be one of the greats. But he gets hurt a lot because of his all-out style of play. It would help him if he could get off the Astroturf." (KH)

Eric Davis plays baseball with a rare combination of all-around skills. In his first four complete seasons, playing for the Cincinnati Reds, he has averaged more than 30 home runs, 90 RBI, and 90 runs scored. Davis stole a remarkable 80 bases in 1986; plagued by knee and ankle injuries, he hasn't matched those numbers in subsequent seasons. A brilliant center fielder known for his spectacular leaping catches against the outfield fence, Davis led NL outfielders in total chances with 394 in 1987.

Andre Dawson
(page 43)

"He's a very quiet man, all business on the field. The portrait in this book really shows his game face. It says,

'You're going to have trouble getting me out.' " (KH)

Andre Dawson won the NL Rookie of the Year Award in 1977 with the Montreal Expos. He developed into an All-Star center fielder, winning four consecutive Gold Glove awards (1980-83), and was named the NL Player of the Year by *The Sporting News* in 1981 and 1987. In a 1983 poll conducted by the *New York Times*, major league players voted Dawson the outstanding player in the game. He signed with the Chicago Cubs as a free agent in 1987 and had the most productive year of his career, hitting 49 home runs and driving in 137 runs. For these accomplishments, and despite the Cubs' last-place finish, Dawson won the NL Most Valuable Player Award. A series of knee operations have hampered his recent performance, yet he continues to play at consistently high levels. In 13 years, he has collected 2,037 hits, 319 home runs, 1,131 RBI, and 1,058 runs scored.

Doug DeCinces
(page 126)

"Doug had the unenviable job of trying to replace Brooks Robinson as the Orioles' third baseman. I don't believe there's any man alive who could have done that. Doug went on to become a very dangerous hitter with the California Angels. He was a 'gamer', and I don't think he was ever really given his due." (MF)

For eight years (1977-1984), De-Cinces was one of the most productive third basemen in the game, averaging 20 home runs and 70 RBI. His finest season came in 1982, when he hit a career-high 30 homers, drove in 97 runs, and was named to the AL All-Star Team. DeCinces twice led AL third basemen in assists and total chances.

Len Dykstra
(page 22)

"'Nails' is cocksure, a Pete Rose blood-and-guts player who gets his uniform dirty. He has a knack for the sensational catch." (KH)

Known for his no-holds-barred style of play, as well as for the huge wad of tobacco in his cheek, Dykstra hit .284 for the New York Mets from 1986 to 1988 and averaged nearly 30 stolen bases per season. Despite getting about 430 at bats per year with New York, Dykstra was unhappy with his platoon status in center field. In 1989, he was traded to the Philadelphia Phillies, where he became a full-time player.

Mike Easler
(page 35)

"I played with Mike in the minor leagues when he was 28 years old and I was only 19 or so. He's one of those guys you're happy for when they make the major leagues because they walked the extra mile to get

there. A lot of other guys with more talent have squandered it. Mike got the most out of his talent—and more." (KH)

Signed to a minor league contract in 1969, Mike Easler didn't reach the majors to stay until 1979. Following his rookie season with the Pittsburgh Pirates, Easler batted a career-high .338 in 1980 and became known as "The Hit Man." He hit over .300 in three major league seasons and had his best year with the Boston Red Sox in 1984, when he averaged .318 with 27 home runs and 91 RBI.

Dwight Evans
(page 37)

"Evans has been a thorn in the side of a lot of pitchers. He's always a tough out and always seems to get up for the big series. He uses his front toe as a timing and balancing mechanism for hitting. Now, to me, hitting has always been about timing, and pitching has always been about the disruption of timing. So, whenever a batter has a routine such as Evans's, I try to disrupt that routine. What invariably happens is that he'll step out of the box to try and throw my rhythm off. We play a kind of cat-and-mouse game, a game within a game." (MF)

"Dewey" Evans's long and distinguished career has two distinct periods. During his first nine seasons, he averaged .265 with 17 home runs and 64 RBI. In the last eight, he joined the game's elite, averaging .280 with 26 homers and

105 RBI per year—a 50 percent increase in home runs and a 65 percent jump in RBI. By the end of the 1989 season, Evans had totaled 366 homers and 1,283 RBI. He is the only player to hit 20 or more home runs in each of the last nine years. One of the finest right fielders of his generation, Evans is known for his game-saving catches and for his powerful and accurate throwing arm.

Rollie Fingers
(page 79)

"Fingers had the perfect reliever's mentality. He was a pitcher who could have a bad day, shake it off, and come back and be effective the next day. Fingers threw quality strikes. He had pinpoint control and lived on the corners. He could wear out those corners.

"Fingers was a guy who literally took over the mound and dictated the pace of the game. You know, when your ace reliever comes in, it means your team is in trouble, that the offense is in a position to score a lot of runs. But when Fingers came in, his mere presence on the mound shifted the pressure to the hitters. You knew he wouldn't give in to you, that he wouldn't make a mistake." (MF)

In a wondrous 17-year career (1968-1985), Fingers set the all-time record for saves with 341. As the bullpen stopper for the A's, he played a pivotal role in leading Oakland to three consecutive World Series championships (1972-74). Fingers led his league in saves

three times, establishing a personal record of 37 with the San Diego Padres in 1978. Pitching for the Milwaukee Brewers in 1981, Fingers saved 28 games and had an ERA of 1.04, becoming the first relief pitcher to win both the Most Valuable Player and Cy Young awards in the same year. Eminently recognizable for his waxed handlebar mustache, Fingers fashioned a lifetime 2.90 ERA, and owns the AL Championship Series record for most saves with 11.

Carlton Fisk
(page 30)

"You can build a whole lineup around Fisk. He likes to take over the pace of the game and seems to draw attention to himself. It's intentional. He aggravates the hitters, he aggravates opposing managers, and I'm sure he aggravates the umpires. But the point is that he's getting his pitchers to concentrate on every pitch. He's trying to make sure that nothing's done that isn't planned. It's hard to fault his success. I think he's destined for the Hall of Fame. And he's handsome—for a catcher." (MF)

The career of the durable, consistent Fisk is studded with remarkable achievements. AL Rookie of the Year in 1972, he was the heart of the 1975 Boston Red Sox team that lost a memorable World Series to the Cincinnati Reds. He hit one of the most dramatic home runs in history to win the sixth game of that Series.

Signed by the Chicago White

Sox as a free agent in 1981, Fisk has continued to play at an all-star pace. In 1985, he set an AL career record for most games caught (1,838) and the single-season home-run standard for a catcher (33). At the age of 41, when most catchers have been retired for 10 years, Fisk led his AL counterparts in RBI and doubles. He holds the AL record for most home runs by a catcher with 315 and has hit a total of 336 (21 when not catching). Fisk has driven in 1,166 runs in his 18 seasons.

Mike Flanagan
(page 69)

"He's a gutsy pitcher. Some pitchers are afraid to throw strikes. They're so afraid a hitter might hit it—in the same way that hitters, when they're in bad slumps, are afraid to swing the bat because they might make an out. Mike Flanagan, I can tell you, has never been afraid to throw strikes. It's obvious he's a guy who has great confidence in his ability."
(Dwight Evans)

The winner of 163 major league games, Mike Flanagan did his best work with the Baltimore Orioles from 1977 to 1983. Omitting the strike-shortened season of 1981, Flanagan averaged 17 wins per year during that time. His finest season came in 1979, when he led in the major leagues with 23 wins, tied for the lead in shutouts with five, and won the AL Cy Young Award.

Julio Franco
(page 85)

"He's got a very strange batting stance—he wraps the bat around his head. I can't believe a person could hit .200 out of that stance, yet Julio is a .300 hitter who drives in a lot of runs. He looks thin and uses a huge bat, so to me he looks like he'd be an easy out. I'm not sure how he does it. He's just a very gifted athlete, an uncanny hitter." (MF)

Traded from the Cleveland Indians to the Texas Rangers in 1989, Franco had the best season of his career, batting .316, with 21 stolen bases, 13 homers, and 92 RBI. At age 28, after seven full seasons, Franco is averaging .298 with 75 RBI per year and 1,232 base hits—superior numbers for a second baseman. Franco is one of many fine infielders to come from the village of San Pedro de Macorís in the Dominican Republic.

Steve Garvey
(pages 46, 59)

"Garvey's only about 5'9", but he's got massive arms. He's built like a little fire hydrant. He's one of the players I truly miss watching. Garvey's one of baseball's great clutch hitters—a game-on-the-line kind of guy." (KH)

Steve Garvey was not only a great talent, but a man of great will, an "iron man" who, in eight seasons, played 1,207 consecutive games—an NL record. In his 19 years with the Dodgers and Padres, Garvey hit .294 with 272 home runs, 1,308 RBI, 1,143 runs scored, and 2,599 base hits. He reached his peak in the four-year period from 1977 to 1980 when he hit .308 and averaged 27 home runs, 111 RBI, and nearly 200 hits per season. Garvey's post-season statistics are equally remarkable: a lifetime .356 batting average in 22 NL Championship Series games and a .319 average in 28 World Series games. In the field, Garvey set records at first base for the fewest errors in a season (0) and for the highest lifetime fielding percentage for a first baseman (.996). On April 16, 1988, Garvey's number "6" was the first to be retired by the Padres in the team's 20-year history.

Dwight Gooden
(pages 80, 105)

"Watching him pitch is like watching a ballet; his body and arms and legs are so synchronized. Watching him pitch is like watching a stream go by; everything is so fluid. And Doc's a great eater, too. Man can he eat. He's one of the biggest eaters I've ever seen. He'll have to watch that when he gets older." (KH)

In 1984, at the age of 19, "Doc" Gooden was named NL Rookie of the Year when he won 17 games and struck out 276 batters. He not only set a record for strikeouts by a rookie pitcher, but was the first teenager to lead the league in that category. In 1985, he became the youngest ever to win the Cy Young Award. By the end of the 1989 season, Gooden, then 24, had become the youngest pitcher in modern baseball history to record 100 victories. His 1,168 career strikeouts also set a record for his age group.

Rich 'Goose' Gossage
(page 109)

"Goose is what a reliever is supposed to be. He throws the ball so hard that he's intimidating—a true closer. I can still see Thurman Munson behind the plate and him and Gossage using no signs at all. It was like they were playing an elevated game of catch." (MF)

One of the game's best relief pitchers, Gossage ranks second in baseball history with 307 saves. He led the AL in saves three times and was named the AL Fireman of the Year in 1975 and 1978 by *The Sporting News*. In six World Series appearances with the New York Yankees in 1978 and 1981, Gossage did not allow a single earned run. He has been named to nine All-Star teams.

Mike Greenwell
(page 28)

"He follows in the tradition of the good Boston hitters: patient, yet aggressive. His strength is that he can hit any pitch, so there's no particular way to pitch him, and that's the highest compliment you can give to a hitter. He's up there in Don Mattingly's class, and he just has to pass the test of time." (MF)

Over the past 50 years, Boston Red Sox left fielders from Ted Williams to Carl Yastrzemski to Jim Rice have established a legacy of excellence. Mike Greenwell seems a worthy heir to that tradition. Nicknamed "Gator," the 26-year-old is fast establishing himself as one of the best all-around hitters in the game. As the Red Sox left fielder for three full seasons, Greenwell has hit over .300 each year with a career average of .319. He is averaging 100 RBI and 35 doubles per year.

Alfredo Griffin
(page 139)

"Griffin is the only player I asked to pose whose face and number I didn't recognize. I was simply drawn to him, especially to his eyes, which suggested a man of great depth and feeling. I was pleased to find out that Griffin was not only a fine portrait subject,

but a player with substantial credentials." (John Weiss)

Alfredo Griffin was voted the AL Co-Rookie of the Year in 1979. He hit .287 that year as the Toronto Blue Jays' shortstop. In 1982, he led AL shortstops with 824 total chances, and in 1983, he led in putouts with 280. As a member of the Oakland A's, Griffin played in the 1984 AL All-Star game; in 1985, he won the Gold Glove Award. Traded to the Dodgers, Griffin was Los Angeles' shortstop in the 1988 World Series.

Tony Gwynn
(page 61)

"I met him at the All-Star game and he's got kind of a pudgy body. I was really surprised. That's not to say he's fat, but he wasn't this well-cut person with a washboard stomach. But he's by far the best hitter in the NL, and that's why he's averaged over .330 for eight years. He stays within himself, hits the ball where it's pitched, hits line drives, and doesn't try to hit home runs." (KH)

The grand master of NL hitters, Gwynn has won the batting title four times, including the last three in a row. His lifetime .332 average is by far the NL's best in the 1980s. Despite Gwynn's less-than-sleek build, he has stolen 221 bases in his eight-year career and averaged 40 during the last four years. Once considered only an adequate defensive player, Gwynn has developed into an All-Star fielder who, in 1989, was awarded a Gold Glove. Gwynn

won the 1989 batting championship on the last day of the season, and is the first to win it in three consecutive years since Stan Musial in 1950, 1951, and 1952.

Keith Hernandez
(page 19)

"Keith brought a new style of play to first base. What he's done is to bring the aggressiveness of a shortstop to a position where they used to park slow fat guys. Batting or fielding, pressure seems to bring out the best in him." (Tom Herr)

Hernandez has established new standards of excellence for playing first base. He received 11 consecutive Gold Glove awards from 1978 to 1988. Though slowed by injuries during the last two seasons, Hernandez has a lifetime .298 batting average with 2,156 hits and 1,063 RBI. He has hit .300 or better six times in his career, reaching a high of .344 in 1979 when he led the majors in hitting. Hernandez was co-recipient of the NL Most Valuable Player Award in 1979, leading the NL in doubles (48) and runs scored (116).

Orel Hershiser
(pages 9, 58, 99)

"He's got great stuff, great command of his stuff, but most of all, he's got guts." (KH)

A late bloomer, Hershiser has won 98 games since his debut in 1984, averaging more than 16 wins per year and winning more than 60 percent of his games. He has never had a losing season. Over the last four years, he has become the ace of the Dodgers staff, pitching more than 230 innings per year. In 1988, Hershiser had one of the most singular successes in baseball history. He set a major league record by pitching 59 straight scoreless innings, led the NL in shutouts with eight, and led the Dodgers to a World Series Championship. For his achievements, he was named the NL Cy Young Award winner and the Most Valuable Player in the World Series.

Al Holland
(page 91)

"Holland was a closer, a one-pitch pitcher, like Al Hrabosky. But when these guys lose their fastballs, they go quickly. There was no one better than Al for about three years. Once he lost his gas and started having to throw breaking balls, he was in trouble." (KH)

Al Holland had two brilliant seasons with the Philadelphia Phillies, saving 25 games in 1983 and 29 in 1984. As the Phils' bullpen stopper, he was instrumental in leading them to the 1983 NL pennant. During that season, Holland struck out 100 batters in 91 innings and gave up only 63 hits. Before and after his two magical seasons, he never recorded more than seven saves per year.

Kent Hrbek
(pages 76, 100, 106)

"I don't think that Kent has ever gotten his due in baseball. He's an unsung first baseman who, very quietly and effectively, gets the job done." (MF)

In a league populated with outstanding first basemen, Hrbek has produced consistently high numbers for both average and power. In eight full seasons with the Minnesota Twins, he has hit .290, averaging 25 homers and 91 RBI per season. He has batted over .300 in three different seasons, hitting 20 or more home runs in his last six consecutive years. Hrbek slugged his 200th major league home run in 1989.

Wally Joyner
(pages 131, 133)

"One of the prettiest swings you'll

ever see in the game, right up there with Brett's and Mattingly's." (MF)

Wally Joyner burst onto the scene as a 23-year-old rookie in 1986. He hit 22 home runs and drove in 100, becoming the 15th player in history to make the AL All-Star Team as a rookie. A model of consistency, Joyner has averaged .288 with 21 home runs and 95 RBI per season.

Fred Lynn
(page 81)

"When Freddy Lynn signed with the Orioles, the knock on him was that he'd only play in 120 games, and that he'd be hurt for 40. And sure enough, that's what happened. When Fred's healthy, he only knows one way to play the game, and that's full speed ahead, Katie-bar-the-door. The problem is, he's always jumping into outfield walls. The Orioles begged him not to play so aggressively. He was hitting those walls with such force that he bent the steel posts behind the fence. A healthy Freddy Lynn plays with reckless abandon, and I have a tremendous amount of respect for that." (MF)

In 1975, with the Boston Red Sox, Lynn had one of the most extraordinary rookie seasons in baseball history, becoming the only player to win both the AL Rookie of the Year and Most Valuable Player awards in the same season. In addition to hitting .331 with 21 homers and 105 RBI, Lynn's center-field play earned him a Gold Glove. Lynn's finest season came in 1979 when he won the AL batting title

(.333) and achieved personal bests in home runs (39) and RBI (122). In his 16-year career, the nine-time All-Star has hit 300 home runs and driven in 1,088 runs.

Dennis Martinez
(page 84)

"He's had a lot of ups and downs in his career. I think he's always suffered because of the problems in Nicaragua. It put a strain on him; he had to become a kind of spokesman for his country, so he had a much bigger burden on his shoulders than the average player. I give him a lot of credit. After playing a long time and getting better, he's truly coming into his own. He can be as good as he wants to be." (MF)

"He has a very awkward pitching motion, a very strange one, like a snake coiling and springing out." (KH)

Dennis Martinez has won 153 big-league games, mostly while pitching for the Baltimore Orioles. Playing for the Montreal Expos in the last three seasons, he has compiled a 42-24 record, winning a remarkable 64 percent of his games. Martinez' 16-7 record in 1989 marked the fifth time in his career that he had won 15 or more games.

Mark McGwire
(page 141)

"McGwire has what is probably the most perfect home-run swing you'll ever see. If a pitcher makes a mistake on the inside of the plate, he's going to hit it a long, long way." (MF)

In only three seasons, McGwire has established himself as one of the great power hitters in the game. He is one of two players in history to hit 30 or more homers in each of his first three seasons (the other was his teammate Jose Canseco). In 1987, McGwire hit 49 home runs and was unanimously selected AL Rookie of the Year. He has driven in 104 runs per year, and with a total of 117 home runs, he has smacked one in every 14.1 times at bat.

Paul Molitor
(pages 33, 144)

"Certain players tend to play borderline out-of-control, and that defines the way Paul Molitor plays baseball. He's a hard-nosed player who's made himself into one of the great hitters in the game." (MF)

A 12-year veteran, Molitor is one of the game's more versatile players, having played second, third, shortstop, and outfield. A lifetime .300

hitter, Molitor has batted over .300 for the last three consecutive seasons and a total of six times in his career. He has also accounted for 1,751 hits and scored 989 runs, impressive statistics considering that in seven of his twelve seasons, he has missed at least 25 percent of his games. Molitor has stolen more than 300 bases and was named the AL Rookie Player of the Year in 1978 by *The Sporting News*.

Jack Morris
(page 129)

"What impresses me about Jack Morris is that he'll never give in. Even when he doesn't have his best stuff, he'll battle you and will somehow get the job done, game after game, season after season." (MF)

Jack Morris, without a lot of fanfare, has won 162 games in the 1980s—more than any other pitcher. In his 13-year career, Morris has pitched 2,794 innings and won a total of 183 games. He won 15 or more games in seven consecutive seasons (1982-88), and has twice been a 20-game winner. Morris had his best season in 1986, when he recorded a 21-8 mark and led the AL with six shutouts. A workhorse, Morris led the Detroit Tigers in innings pitched for 10 straight years from 1979 to 1988, averaging well over 200 innings per season. In 1981, *The Sporting News* named him Pitcher of the Year.

Phil Niekro
(pages 38, 74, 93)

"He looks like Kirk Douglas. You never wanted to face him, even if you were red-hot. He could put you into a slump in a hurry." (KH)

Phil Niekro endured a long apprenticeship, spending part or all of each season from 1959 to 1966 in the Braves' farm system. In his first full season, in 1967, he led the NL with a 1.87 ERA. Twenty years later, the great knuckleballer retired with 318 major league victories, including three 20-win seasons and 13 years with 15 or more victories. Pitching almost his entire career for Atlanta, Niekro appeared in 864 games, pitched more than 5,400 innings, and struck out over 3,300 batters. On October 8, 1985, at the age of 45, Niekro became the oldest pitcher ever to hurl a shutout with an 8-0, four-hit win for the Yankees over Toronto. The shutout, his 45th, was also his 300th victory.

Dave Parker
(page 121)

"In the late seventies, he was the best player in the game. He could do it all—throw, field, hit with power, hit in the clutch. He'd just put this massive body up against you—and he had this loud, boisterous personality, which

made him the most intimidating hitter I've ever seen in my career." (KH)

In 17 major league seasons, Parker has established himself as one of his generation's great hitters. He has smashed 307 homers among his more than 2,400 hits, knocking in 1,342 runs and scoring 1,154. Parker has hit over .300 six times, including five consecutive years from 1975 to 1979. He led the NL in batting twice, in 1977 and 1978, with averages of .338 and .334. Parker was named the NL Most Valuable Player in 1978 while playing for the Pittsburgh Pirates. That same year, he won his second consecutive batting title while hitting 30 home runs and driving in 117. Traded to the Reds in 1984, Parker averaged 27 home runs and 108 RBI during his four years with Cincinnati. He has spent the last two seasons with the A's, and in 1989, at the age of 38, he hit 22 homers and drove in 97 runs.

Lance Parrish
(page 103)

"A fine, all-around catcher who combines power hitting and defensive skills. He's been troubled by a bad back for the last few years, and I think that's all that's prevented him from putting up Hall of Fame numbers." (MF)

Lance Parrish, the Detroit Tigers' catcher from 1977 to 1986, ranks among the finest to play his position. He has hit over 30 home runs twice in his career, and for the five-year period from 1982 to 1986, he

averaged 28 homers per season. A six-time AL All-Star, Parrish won six Gold Gloves for defensive excellence. He has a total of 261 lifetime home runs and has driven in 877.

Tony Perez
(page 94)

"One of the truly great clutch hitters of his era. He and Steve Garvey are two of the best ever." (KH)

As a major contributor to the great "Big Red Machine" teams of the 1970s, Perez helped put Cincinnati into four World Series. For 11 consecutive seasons (1967-1977), he knocked in 90 or more runs per year. He had his finest season in 1970 with career bests in home runs (40), RBI (129), runs scored (107), and batting average (.317). In his 20-year career, Perez amassed 379 home runs and 1,652 RBI. He appeared in eight All-Star games and ranks 14th on the all-time RBI list. Every player with more RBI than Perez has been elected to the Hall of Fame.

Kirby Puckett
(page 53)

"He's become the premier center fielder in the American League. He's a very dangerous, unpredictable hitter. There's no way to pitch him. He's a

bad ball hitter. He's had hits off me on balls that bounced before they reached the plate. I've seen him hit balls pitched over his head, pitches thrown faster than 90 miles per hour. He comes to the plate anxious to hit, takes one quick practice swing, and seems to say, 'O.K., come on, throw it in here.' " (MF)

Kirby Puckett may be the game's greatest all-around player. He had 200 or more hits in each of the last four years, and is averaging 207 hits per year in his six seasons with the Minnesota Twins. Puckett's proportions—5'8", 210 pounds—would not suggest that he is one of the great acrobatic center fielders of his time, yet he is known for his astounding, leaping catches against and above the Metrodome's outfield barrier. An entertaining and popular player, Puckett has a lifetime batting average of .323. He has established personal bests with a .356 average (1988), 121 RBI (1988), and 31 home runs (1986). In 1989, Puckett hit .339 to win the AL batting championship.

Tim Raines
(page 68)

"Raines is the next-best hitter to Tony Gwynn in the National League." (KH)

The switch-hitting Tim "Rock" Raines is one of the great leadoff hitters in baseball. Named NL Rookie Player of the Year by *The Sporting News* in 1981, Raines has a .303 career average, including four straight years of hitting .300 or better (1984-87). One of the great

base stealers in the game, Raines has swiped almost 600 bags; six years in a row, he stole 70 or more. At the end of the 1989 season, he was the all-time major league leader in successful steals with 87 percent. Raines has averaged 100 runs scored per season over the last eight years. His best season was 1983, when he led the league with 133 runs scored.

Willie Randolph
(page 47)

"The only way to describe Willie Randolph is to call him a pest. He's so aggravating to pitch against. He takes forever to get set, stepping in and out of the batter's box. He takes a lot of pitches, works the count in his favor, and invariably, it seems, he gets a walk or a hit. And then he causes a lot of havoc on the bases." (MF)

A quality second baseman respected for doing all the little things it takes to win ball games, Randolph played 14 years with the New York Yankees. Randolph's lifetime average is .274, and in 1987, his finest season, he hit .305 and scored 96 runs. He led AL second basemen in double plays in 1979 and 1984, and was named to *The Sporting News* AL All-Star Team three times. Signed as a free agent by the Los Angeles Dodgers, he hit .282 in 1989.

Jim Rice
(page 112)

"A classic power hitter, Jim Rice has a compact stroke and generates tremendous power. I've actually seen him check his swing and break his bat!" (MF)

Rice has led the AL in home runs three times, cracking a total of 382 in 15 seasons. He had a storybook year in 1978, winning the AL Most Valuable Player Award and leading the league in hits (213), home runs (46), triples (15), RBI (139), and slugging percentage (.600). For good measure, he hit .315. Rice has a total of 2,452 career hits, along with a .298 average and 1,451 RBI.

Cal Ripken, Jr.
(pages 125, 143, 147)

"He's an imposing physical talent, probably the biggest shortstop ever to play the game, but where he separates himself from others is in his mental approach to the game. He's a thinking man's shortstop, and he's got tremendous baseball instincts. I think he's a Hall of Fame-type player— one of a kind." (MF)

Only 29 years old and already a nine-year veteran, Ripken has played in 1,250 consecutive games, third on the all-time list behind the

legendary Lou Gehrig (2,130 games) and the obscure Everett "Deacon" Scott (1,307 games), a little-known shortstop who played from 1914 to 1926. It is believed that Ripken's streak of 8,243 consecutive innings, from May 30, 1982 to September 14, 1987, is the longest of its kind in baseball history. The streak ended in Toronto in the eighth inning of an 18-3 loss to the Blue Jays. The manager of the Orioles that season was Cal Ripken, Sr.

Cal Jr. was AL Rookie of the Year in 1982 and the Most Valuable Player in 1983. He established the AL record for most assists by a shortstop (583) in 1984, and has led the league in double plays three times. He is the first shortstop in history to hit 20 or more home runs in eight straight seasons.

Pete Rose
(page 89)

"Pete Rose is the greatest charismatic figure that I've ever seen on a baseball field." (KH)

For 24 years, Rose's hard-driving, incessant style made America's baseball pulse quicken. By force of will alone, it seemed, he made himself into the dominant player of his time. His accomplishments spill out of record books, but none is more remarkable than his record for most hits in the history of baseball: 4,256. Fifteen times Rose batted over .300, including nine consecutive seasons from 1965 to 1973. He owns the record for most games played (3,562), most seasons with 200 or more hits (10), most seasons with 100 or more hits (23), most seasons playing in 100 or more games (23), and most winning games played (1,972). Rose is the only player in history to play 500 or more games at each of five different positions. He set a modern NL record in 1978 by hitting in 44 straight games. In 1989, in his fifth season as manager of the Cincinnati Reds, Pete Rose was banned from baseball for alleged gambling activities.

Nolan Ryan
(page 122)

"Nolan Ryan is the most intimidating pitcher of my generation, a typical Texan. He'll strut around that mound, toss his shoulders back and forth like a cowboy—which he is—and look back at you like he's in Abilene having a gunfight, ready to draw on you, squared off and facing you down at 60 paces." (KH)

While most flamethrowing fastballers burn out in their early thirties, Nolan Ryan at 42 throws as hard as he did 20 years ago. He won 16 games in 1989, striking out 301 batters in 239 innings and allowing the opposition only 162 hits. Ryan has had 300 or more strikeouts in six seasons and 200 or more in thirteen. His total of 5,076 strikeouts is not merely the best in history, it dwarfs other totals. Ryan has won 289 games, pitched 4,786 innings, and given up only 3,492 hits. He has thrown five no-hit games, the most in history, and set the record for

most strikeouts in a season with 383 in 1973. Ryan's fastball has been timed at over 100 miles per hour.

Juan Samuel
(page 72)

"He plays at 100 miles per hour every day, every game. He's a very serious, inward person, but a nice man, too. He doesn't show his emotions, he hides them. I never know what's going on inside him, so he's really kind of a curiosity to me." (KH)

Samuel was named *The Sporting News* NL Rookie Player of the Year in 1984, a season in which he became only the third second baseman in history to collect 80 extra-base hits. From 1984 to 1987, Samuel averaged 35 doubles, 15 triples, 20 home runs, and 51 stolen bases, the first player in baseball history to have double figures in all four categories in his first four seasons. As the Phillies' second baseman, Samuel was twice selected for the NL All-Star Team. In 1989, he was shifted to center field, and later that season was traded to the Mets.

Ryne Sandberg
(page 137)

"Ryne might be offended by this, but he kind of reminds me of 'Baby Face' Nelson. He's got this sweet, youthful,

good-looking face, a disarming face, but he's lethal with a bat in his hands. And nobody turns a double play better than he does." (KH)

Sandberg set a major league record at second base in 1989 when he played in 90 consecutive games without an error. He also became the first second baseman in 30 years to hit 30 home runs in a season. Since he reached the majors to stay in 1982, only Dale Murphy and Cal Ripken, Jr. have had more at bats. The Most Valuable Player in the NL in 1984, Sandberg hit .314 with 19 home runs and led the league in triples and runs scored. In his eight-year career, Sandberg averages 94 runs, 31 stolen bases, and 28 doubles per year. He has been selected for the last six All-Star teams.

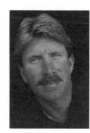

Mike Schmidt
(page 88)

"Everyone forgets the days when Mike Schmidt was hitting .250 and striking out 150 times a season. He made himself into a great hitter, but I'm more amazed by his longevity. He maintained such a high standard of excellence by keeping himself in great shape. When he retired, he had the same physique as when he was 30." (KH)

Mike Schmidt was the greatest hitter ever to play third base, and arguably the greatest fielder as well. Before retiring in May 1989, when he could no longer perform at his own high standard, Schmidt had won a record eight NL home-run

titles and 10 Gold Glove awards for defensive excellence. He finished his career with 548 home runs, placing him seventh on the all-time list, and he holds the single-season record for most home runs by a third baseman (48). His 1595 RBI rank him seventeenth in history and first among third basemen. Along with Stan Musial and Roy Campanella, Schmidt is one of only three players to win the NL Most Valuable Player Award three times. In 1980, Schmidt led the Philadelphia Phillies to a World Series Championship and was selected as the Series' Most Valuable Player.

Tom Seaver
(page 113)

"He's the Dean, the philosopher of pitchers, the master of mechanics. Tom presents a kind of preppy front that hides the fact that he's really a practical joker. That's a side of him very few people see and the side I like the most. Getting to know Seaver's real personality has been one of the great surprises of my career. I really consider him a good friend." (KH)

In his illustrious 20-year career, Seaver compiled a 311-205 pitching record, winning more than 60 percent of his games. Seaver's 3,640 strikeouts placed him third in history, and he was eighth in shutouts with 61. Seaver established major league records for most seasons with 200 or more strikeouts (10) and most consecutive seasons with 200 or more strikeouts (9). The winner of 20 or more games five times in his career, Seaver won at least 15 games during 13 different seasons. Pitching primarily for the New York Mets, he won three NL Cy Young awards.

Ken Singleton
(pages 75, 111)

"What I remember most about Ken was the great year he had in 1979, when he hit 35 home runs and 19 of them were hit in games I pitched. He was 6'4" or 6'5", but had a keen eye at the plate. As a matter of fact, he led off for the Orioles. And I don't think there's ever been a larger lead-off hitter in the game. He was a student of the game and taught a lot of us about the art of baseball. One of the true gentlemen I've played with." (MF)

The switch-hitting Ken Singleton was an outstanding all-around hitter. He collected 2,029 career hits to go along with a .282 average, 246 home runs, and 1,065 RBI. In 14 seasons, Singleton worked major league pitchers for an average of 90 or more walks per year. His finest seasons were from 1977 to 1980, when he averaged .305 with 26 homers and 99 RBI. A highly effective post-season player, Singleton hit .321 in two AL Championship Series and .345 in two World Series.

Dave Smith
(page 64)

"He's one of the great stoppers. A stopper has to be a different breed of cat because he faces pressure situations all the time. Smith will walk some guys, get himself into a jam, and then get out of it. He's one of those pitchers who'll give you a heart attack." (KH)

Dave Smith had 24 or more saves during each of his last five seasons and a total of 176 saves in his 10-year career with the Houston Astros. In 1988, he became the 12th reliever in history to reach 150 saves; in 1986, he set a personal record of 33 in a season. His lifetime ERA is under 3.00.

Ozzie Smith
(page 11)

"There's no question that he's by far the best fielder in the league—hands down, the best player defensively. But he doesn't get enough credit for his offense. He is the most improved player, offensively, that I've seen in my 15 years. He does all the little things it takes to win a ball game. He's one of the top three situation hitters in the league." (KH)

Osborne Earl Smith, a.k.a. the "Wizard of Oz," is renowned for his incredible range at shortstop and for his acrobatic skills. He was awarded a Gold Glove in every season of the 1980s. His fielding records include most consecutive years leading the NL in assists for a shortstop (4) and most years leading in fielding average (6). Smith's improvement as an offensive threat is easily documented. In his first seven seasons, his batting average was only .238. In his last five, he has averaged .281, ranking with the leading hitters at his position. Smith has scored a career total of 849 runs and has stolen 432 bases, averaging 36 per year. The slight (5'10", 155 lb.) shortstop is also one of the game's most durable players; in nine of his twelve major league seasons, he has played in 150 or more games.

Dave Stewart
(page 49)

"I have a lot of respect for Dave Stewart. He was almost out of baseball at one time. He always seemed to have great ability, and yet he struggled for a long time. A number of organizations gave up on him. They tried everything to help him break through because of the great ability he had. Sometimes 'great ability' is a curse; your skill is so great that you don't learn how to pitch. But now, after all those hard years, he's had his third straight 20-win season: an amazing accomplishment. He's really turned his career around." (MF)

In Dave Stewart's first six big-league seasons, he played for three different teams and had a record of 39-40. In the last three years, pitching for the Oakland A's, Stewart has won more games than any of his contemporaries, compiling a record of 62-34. The only man in the majors to win 20 or more games each year in this period, Stewart has become the backbone of the Oakland staff, pitching an average of 265 innings a season. With two victories and a 1.69 ERA, Stewart was voted the Most Valuable Player in the 1989 World Series.

Darryl Strawberry
(page 23)

"Darryl's under huge pressure in New York with all the expectations. He's supposed to be the next Ted Williams and the next Willie McCovey wrapped into one. He's really quite a misunderstood person, and a really fine man." (KH)

In 1988, at the age of 26, Strawberry became the New York Mets' all-time home-run leader. By the end of 1989, Strawberry had already hit 215 home runs and collected 625 RBI while averaging 25 stolen bases per season. Strawberry won the NL Rookie of the Year Award in 1983 when he hit 26 homers and drove in 74 runs. He had superb back-to-back seasons in 1987 and 1988 with 39 home runs and over 100 RBI each year.

Don Sutton
(page 52)

"I've always had an appreciation for Don Sutton. I enjoyed watching him on the mound, trying to figure out what he was going to throw, when he was going to throw it, and why he would throw a certain pitch. He was one of those pitchers who could dominate a game. And you always knew he was out there; he drew attention to himself. He was not only a master on the mound, he had a mystique." (MF)

In a remarkable 23-year career, mostly with the Los Angeles Dodgers, Don Sutton won 324 games and set a record by striking out 100 or more batters in 21 consecutive years. He ranks fourth all-time in career strikeouts (3,574), and sixth in innings pitched (5,280). Sutton thought of himself as a mechanic on the pitcher's mound, tinkering and fiddling with his pitching controls to keep hitters off balance. Many hitters believed that Sutton's most effective adjustment was scuffing the ball, making it dance and hop like a Wiffle ball. When he retired in 1988, Sutton ranked eighth in career shutouts with 58.

Kent Tekulve
(page 71)

"Ray Bolger on the hill. He was the top reliever in the NL in the late seventies and early eighties. I always bummed cigarettes off him. When he was in the dugout and I was on the field, he'd tease me by showing me a pack of Winstons or Marlboros." (KH)

Kent Tekulve was a stringbean righthander (6'4", 190 lbs.) with an underhand "submarine" pitching style. He didn't make the major leagues until he was 27 years old, but by the time he retired in 1989, he had pitched in 1,050 games, the all-time record for appearances by a relief pitcher. In 1987, at the age of 40, Tekulve relieved in 90 games, becoming the oldest pitcher in NL history to lead in that category. Pitching primarily for the Pittsburgh Pirates, Tekulve saved a total of 184 games and finished his career ranked ninth in saves.

Garry Templeton
(page 24)

"Next to Darryl Strawberry, he's the finest talent that I've ever seen come up from the minor leagues. Injuries to his knees have really limited what he can do. He's a fantastic guy, a good friend, and a smart player." (KH)

In 1979, Garry Templeton became the first switch hitter to collect 100 or more hits from each side of the plate in a single season. In Templeton's first full year, at the age of 21, he became the youngest shortstop in modern baseball history to reach 200 hits and only the 14th shortstop ever to reach that mark. In that same 1977 season, Templeton finished second in the NL batting race with a .322 average. Traded from the St. Louis Cardinals to the San Diego Padres, he led NL shortstops in runs scored and RBI in 1982. Templeton had surgery performed on his left knee in 1983 and never again approached the brilliance of his earlier years. In his first six seasons, Templeton hit .305, but has averaged only .253 in the last eight.

Andre Thornton
(page 51)

"For years he was the major threat in the Indians lineup. He was a very patient hitter with a short, compact swing. And somehow, he had a sixth sense for knowing what pitch was coming. He was always a class act, both on and off the field." (MF)

Andre Thornton hit 253 career home runs and had 895 RBI. He hit 30 or more homers three times and had his most productive season in 1982 with the Cleveland Indians, when he hit 32 home runs, knocked in 116, scored 90 runs, and walked 109 times. From 1977 to 1987, Thornton ranked sixth in the AL for home runs per times at bat (1:20)

and ranked fifth in RBI per at bat (1:5.76). A two-time AL All-Star, Thornton retired in 1987 as the Indians' top right-handed home-run hitter with 214.

Fernando Valenzuela
(page 21)

"He's a charismatic pitcher, someone who captured the imagination of America. He reminds me of a left-handed Juan Marichal. With the bases loaded, he can throw you any one of three different types of screwballs for a perfect strike. He's the type of guy that I love to watch pitch: a master who can work the corners with different pitches, and is unpredictable in any situation." (KH)

"Fernandomania" swept the country during Valenzuela's rookie season in 1981, when he led the Los Angeles Dodgers to a World Series. In his sensational first year, Valenzuela was NL Rookie of the Year and won the Cy Young Award. He finished that strike-shortened season with a 13-7 record and led the NL with 8 shutouts, 11 complete games, 192 innings pitched, and 180 strikeouts. In Valenzuela's first eight seasons, he had a record of 113-82. Slowed by arm injuries in 1988-89, he lost 21 games and won only 15.

Lou Whitaker
(page 31)

"Lou is a thoroughly professional baseball player. He's a battler and a perennial All-Star. He's not that big, only 160 pounds or so. When you face him in the batter's box, you think he can't hit the ball even 280 feet, and all of a sudden he'll mash one 400 feet into the upper deck." (MF)

Alongside Alan Trammell, Lou Whitaker helped form the premier double-play combination in the AL for the last decade. Always a threat as a hitter, Whitaker has amassed 1,719 hits in his career. He has hit .285 or better five times, and had a career-high .320 batting average in 1983. In 1989, Whitaker generated the best power numbers of his career, belting 28 homers and knocking in 85 runs. He has scored nearly 1,000 career runs and has played in four AL All-Star games.

Dave Winfield
(page 27)

"He's one of the most physically imposing players I've ever seen—he takes up the whole batter's box. He's capable of hitting any pitch, so there's no way to set him up. He's one of the few hitters who walks up there and really makes you afraid he may hit it back up the middle." (MF)

Dave Winfield is one of the game's great all-around athletes. At the University of Minnesota, he was drafted not only by the San Diego Padres, but by basketball's Atlanta Hawks and football's Minnesota Vikings. One of a handful of current players who never played in the minor leagues, Winfield had eight productive seasons with a series of poor Padres teams. Signed as a free agent in 1980 by the New York Yankees, Winfield has collected 357 home runs, 1,438 RBI, and 1,314 runs scored in his career. He drove in 100 or more runs in five consecutive seasons (1982-86) and has hit over .300 four times. Winfield's defensive excellence in right field has been recognized with seven Gold Glove awards. A perennial All-Star, Winfield appeared in 12 consecutive All-Star games through 1988.

Robin Yount
(page 87)

"If you were going to make an ideal shortstop or center fielder, you'd probably use Robin Yount as your model. Great hitters are able to adapt to all kinds of pitches throughout their careers, and Robin has proved what a tremendous talent he is by seeming to improve all the time. He is getting very close to Hall of Fame numbers." (MF)

Yount became the Milwaukee Brewers' shortstop in 1974 at the age of 18. Now, 16 years later, he has quietly established himself as one of the game's great players.

Yount's tenure at shortstop lasted 11 seasons, and following arthroscopic shoulder surgery after the 1984 season, he was switched to center field. In 1976, Yount led AL shortstops with 831 total chances; a decade later, in 1986, he led AL outfielders with a .997 fielding percentage. Yount has batted over .300 six times in his career, driven in 80 or more seven times, and scored 90 or more seven times. He has 226 career steals and 2,602 hits. Yount has twice won his league's Most Valuable Player Award, in 1982 and 1989.

Index to Photographs

and player profiles (italics)

ACKNOWLEDGMENTS

A project of this scope, one that lasts more than five years and involves hundreds of people, cannot be owned by just one person. It is, therefore, such a sweet pleasure to acknowledge in print, to thank from the heart, those who helped give this book life. First and foremost, I thank my friend and colleague, the writer KEVIN KERRANE, who encouraged me to begin this adventure and who continues to come to my aid. I am also particularly obliged to my old high school friend RON SHAPIRO, now an attorney and an advisor to professional athletes. For his counsel, and especially for the warm glow of his friendship, my thanks.

I am truly beholden to LARRY SHENK of the Philadelphia Phillies and to ROBERT BROWN and HELEN CONKLIN of the Baltimore Orioles for making it so pleasant to work at Veterans Stadium and at Memorial Stadium. All but three of the photographs in this book were made at those sites. Thanks to the kindness of DICK BRESCIANI and MARY JANE RYAN, the remaining shots were made at Fenway Park, home of the Boston Red Sox. I also wish to thank BILL BECK of the San Diego Padres for his many considerations.

To my assistants, VICKIE PRICKETT and STEVE TOMASKO, whose good work and energy made them such a pleasure to have around, I offer a hug and a handshake.

It has been my singular good fortune to have as my agent RUSSELL GALEN of the Scott Meredith Literary Agency in New York City. Every author should have such a champion on his side. And speaking of champions, my enduring thanks to WILFRID SHEED for joining me in this enterprise and batting clean-up. I also wish to commend the work of my editor, OWEN ANDREWS, for his steady hand in times of stress, for his guidance, for his caring. And thanks also to REBECCA BEALL BARNS for her sharp eye in the editing of the player profiles. I am grateful, too, to MARY ALICE PARSONS and JIM GIBSON, the book's designers, whose talent and support have made a difference. And most particularly of all, I thank JOHN GRANT for taking on this project and having faith in it.

My thanks to JIM HUGHES for pointing me in the right direction. My thanks to BOBBY ZAREM for favors rendered. My thanks for helping to that notorious Mets fan, VINCE GAGLIARDI. And thanks to MICHAEL SCHWARTZ for coming through in the clutch.

To my friend LARRY ROSEN, gifted sportscaster and producer, my gratitude for good advice and quality research. And thanks to HOWARD ESKIN, the controversial but never dull sportscaster, who helped a stranger and made a friend.

I am indebted to my colleagues at the University of Delaware: HELEN GOULDNER, Dean of the College of Arts and Sciences; and MARTHA CAROTHERS, BELENA CHAPP, MILENE JONES, PETER REES, and DANIEL TEIS. Thanks also to my students: KRISTIN FILSON, JON STOVICEK, SUE WINGE, JOHN CORIGLIANO, LEONARD WHITE, ERIC RUSSELL, DAN DELLA PIAZZA, DANA DAGLE-LONG, PAUL ERHARDT, THOMAS JONES, BECKY DIETZ, BEN CRICCHI, and especially JOHN KUBASKA. I also wish to recognize the General University Research Program for a grant which helped greatly in carrying out this project.

Thanks to KENN JONES, JR., for inspiration and support. Thanks to SUSAN DEVINS, WARREN RUBINSTEIN, and JONATHAN JOSEPH RUBENSTEIN. Thanks to STEPHEN PERLOFF and to JIM STONE and to JON SLOBOTKIN. Thanks to E.J. CALLANAN, a future major leaguer. Thanks to ALDO ROMAGNOLI, owner of the Newark Camera Shop, for his dozens of gestures of kindness. Thanks to RON WAXMAN, LYN WATNER, and SUSAN GREIG. Thanks always to JIMMY ANSPACHER, FRANK DOLBEAR, DONALD ERCEG, PAUL FRIEDMAN, FREDERICK SOMMER, and MINOR WHITE.

Special thanks and a wink to NORRIS JONES, the Orioles' Visiting Team Batboy, who could always be counted on to sneak me a bag of sunflower seeds. And thanks to his counterpart in Philadelphia, JOEY DUNN, for making sure I never ran out of bubble gum.

My sincere appreciation goes to MIKE FLANAGAN and KEITH HERNANDEZ for their contributions to the Player Profiles. Thanks to DWIGHT EVANS and TOM HERR for their comments as well.

I want to acknowledge my everlasting debt of gratitude to the players who made time to pose for me, many of them more than once. I give equal thanks to those whose faces grace these pages and to those who were omitted. Those exclusions were due directly to the limits of space—or to my own limits as a photographer.

And, the best for last, my love and appreciation to my daughter, Sara, not only for her encouragement, but for the clarity, fidelity, and insight she brought to an ongoing evaluation of my work.   J.W.